THE JEWISH AMERICANS

THE JEWISH AMERICANS

Howard Muggamin

CHELSEA HOUSE PUBLISHERS

New York   Philadelphia

Cover Photograph: On New York City's Lower East Side around 1905, a boy stands in his *tallith*, a shawl traditionally worn by Jewish males during morning prayers.

Editor-in-Chief: Nancy Toff
Executive Editor: Remmel T. Nunn
Managing Editor: Karyn Gullen Browne
Copy Chief: Juliann Barbato
Picture Editor: Adrian G. Allen
Art Director: Giannella Garrett
Manufacturing Manager: Gerald Levine

Staff for THE JEWISH AMERICANS:
Senior Editor: Sam Tanenhaus
Assistant Editor: Abigail Meisel
Copyeditor: Karen Hammonds
Deputy Copy Chief: Ellen Scordato
Editorial Assistant: Theodore Keyes
Picture Researcher: PAR/NYC
Designer: Noreen M. Lamb
Layout: Ayn Svoboda
Production Coordinator: Joseph Romano
Cover Illustrator: Paul Biniasz
Banner Design: Hrana L. Janto

3 5 7 9 8 6 4 2

Library of Congress Cataloging-in-Publication Data

Muggamin, Howard.
    The Jewish Americans / Howard Muggamin.
        p.   cm. — (The Peoples of North America)
    Bibliography: p.
    Includes index.
    Summary: Discusses the history, culture, and religion of the Jews; factors encouraging
their emigration; and their acceptance as an ethnic group in North America.
    ISBN 0-87754-887-0
            0-7910-0270-5 (pbk.)
        1. Jews—United States—Juvenile literature. 2. United States—Ethnic relations—Juvenile
literature. [1. Jews—United States—History. 2. Ethnic relations.] I. Title. II. Series.
    E184.J5M84 1988   87-32028
    973'.04924—dc19

CONTENTS

THE PEOPLES OF NORTH AMERICA

CHELSEA HOUSE PUBLISHERS

A
NATION
OF
NATIONS

Daniel Patrick Moynihan

The Constitution of the United States begins: "We the People of the United States . . ." Yet, as we know, the United States is not made up of a single group of people. It is made up of many peoples. Immigrants from Europe, Asia, Africa, and Central and South America settled in North America seeking a new life filled with opportunities unavailable in their homeland. Coming from many nations, they forged one nation and made it their own. More than 100 years ago, Walt Whitman expressed this perception of America as a melting pot: "Here is not merely a nation, but a teeming Nation of nations."

Although the ingenuity and acts of courage of these immigrants, our ancestors, shaped the North American way of life, we sometimes take their contributions for granted. This fine series, *The Peoples of North America,* examines the experiences and contributions of the immigrants and how these contributions determined the future of the United States and Canada.

Immigrants did not abandon their ethnic traditions when they reached the shores of North America. Each ethnic group had its own customs and traditions, and each brought different experiences, accomplishments, skills, values, styles of dress, and tastes in food that lingered long after its arrival. Yet this profusion of differences created a singularity, or bond, among the immigrants.

The United States and Canada are unusual in this respect. Whereas religious and ethnic differences have sparked intolerance throughout the rest of the world—from the 17th-century religious wars to the 19th-century nationalist movements in Europe to the near extermination of the Jewish people under Nazi Germany— North Americans have struggled to learn how to respect each other's differences and live in harmony.

Millions of immigrants from scores of homelands brought diversity to our continent. In a mass migration, some 12 million immigrants passed through the waiting rooms of New York's Ellis Island; thousands more came to the West Coast. At first, these immigrants were welcomed because labor was needed to meet the demands of the Industrial Age. Soon, however, the new immigrants faced the prejudice of earlier immigrants who saw them as a burden on the economy. Legislation was passed to limit immigration. The Chinese Exclusion Act of 1882 was among the first laws closing the doors to the promise of America. The Japanese were also effectively excluded by this law. In 1924, Congress set immigration quotas on a country-by-country basis.

Such prejudices might have triggered war, as they did in Europe, but North Americans chose negotiation and compromise, instead. This determination to resolve differences peacefully has been the hallmark of the peoples of North America.

The remarkable ability of Americans to live together as one people was seriously threatened by the issue of slavery. It was a symptom of growing intolerance in the world. Thousands of settlers from the British Isles had arrived in the colonies as indentured servants, agreeing to work for a specified number of years on farms or as apprentices in return for passage to America and room and board. When the first Africans arrived in the then-British colonies during the 17th century, some colonists thought that they too should be treated as indentured servants. Eventually, the question of whether the Africans should be viewed as indentured, like the English, or as slaves who could be owned for life, was considered in a Maryland court. The court's calamitous decree held that blacks were slaves bound to lifelong servitude, and so were their children.

America went through a time of moral examination and civil war before it finally freed African slaves and their descendants. The principle that all people are created equal had faced its greatest challenge and survived.

Yet the court ruling that set blacks apart from other races fanned flames of discrimination that burned long after slavery was abolished—and that still flicker today. The concept of racism had existed for centuries in countries throughout the world. For instance, when the Manchus conquered China in the 13th century, they decreed that Chinese and Manchus could not intermarry. To impress their superiority on the conquered Chinese, the Manchus ordered all Chinese men to wear their hair in a long braid called a queue.

By the 19th century, some intellectuals took up the banner of racism, citing Charles Darwin. Darwin's scientific studies hypothesized that highly evolved animals were dominant over other animals. Some advocates of this theory applied it to humans, asserting that certain races were more highly evolved than others and thus were superior.

This philosophy served as the basis for a new form of discrimination, not only against nonwhite people but also against various ethnic groups. Asians faced harsh discrimination and were depicted by popular 19th-century newspaper cartoonists as depraved, degenerate, and deficient in intelligence. When the Irish flooded American cities to escape the famine in Ireland, the cartoonists caricatured the typical "Paddy" (a common term for Irish immigrants) as an apelike creature with jutting jaw and sloping forehead.

By the 20th century, racism and ethnic prejudice had given rise to virulent theories of a Northern European master race. When Adolf Hitler came to power in Germany in 1933, he popularized the notion of Aryan supremacy. "Aryan," a term referring to the Indo-European races, was applied to so-called superior physical characteristics such as blond hair, blue eyes, and delicate facial features. Anyone with darker and heavier features was considered inferior. Buttressed by these theories, the German Nazi state from

1933 to 1945 set out to destroy European Jews, along with Poles, Russians, and other groups considered inferior. It nearly succeeded. Millions of these people were exterminated.

The tragedies brought on by ethnic and racial intolerance throughout the world demonstrate the importance of North America's efforts to create a society free of prejudice and inequality.

A relatively recent example of the New World's desire to resolve ethnic friction nonviolently is the solution the Canadians found to a conflict between two ethnic groups. A long-standing dispute as to whether Canadian culture was properly English or French resurfaced in the mid-1960s, dividing the peoples of the French-speaking Quebec Province from those of the English-speaking provinces. Relations grew tense, then bitter, then violent. The Royal Commission on Bilingualism and Biculturalism was established to study the growing crisis and to propose measures to ease the tensions. As a result of the commission's recommendations, all official documents and statements from the national government's capital at Ottawa are now issued in both French and English, and bilingual education is encouraged.

The year 1980 marked a coming of age for the United States's ethnic heritage. For the first time, the U.S. Census asked people about their ethnic background. Americans chose from more than 100 groups, including French Basque, Spanish Basque, French Canadian, Afro-American, Peruvian, Armenian, Chinese, and Japanese. The ethnic group with the largest response was English (49.6 million). More than 100 million Americans claimed ancestors from the British Isles, which includes England, Ireland, Wales, and Scotland. There were almost as many Germans (49.2 million) as English. The Irish-American population (40.2 million) was third, but the next largest ethnic group, the Afro-Americans, was a distant fourth (21 million). There was a sizable group of French ancestry (13 million), as well as of Italian (12 million). Poles, Dutch, Swedes, Norwegians, and Russians followed. These groups, and other smaller ones, represent the wondrous profusion of ethnic influences in North America.

Canada, too, has learned more about the diversity of its population. Studies conducted during the French/English conflict showed that Canadians were descended from Ukrainians, Germans, Italians, Chinese, Japanese, native Indians, and Eskimos, among others. Canada found it had no ethnic majority, although nearly half of its immigrant population had come from the British Isles. Canada, like the United States, is a land of immigrants for whom mutual tolerance is a matter of reason as well as principle.

The people of North America are the descendants of one of the greatest migrations in history. And that migration is not over. Koreans, Vietnamese, Nicaraguans, Cubans, and many others are heading for the shores of North America in large numbers. This mix of cultures shapes every aspect of our lives. To understand ourselves, we must know something about our diverse ethnic ancestry. Nothing so defines the North American nations as the motto on the Great Seal of the United States: *E Pluribus Unum*—Out of Many, One. ⬿

Orthodox Jewish boys play during a group outing.

JEWS IN AMERICA

Few ethnic groups or religious minorities have reached this country's shores with a history as long and troubled as that of the Jews. Those who arrived here in the 19th and early 20th centuries could look back on nearly 3,000 years of persecution: They had been enslaved in ancient Egypt in approximately 1000 B.C. and banished from their Palestinian homeland in A.D. 135. Once in exile, Jews scattered across Europe and the Middle East, searching in vain for a country that would welcome them. They found at best fleeting periods of tolerance, often followed by a backlash of anti-Semitic violence.

Despite this adversity, remarkably few European Jews packed their bags and followed other disgruntled groups to North America during the great migrations of the early 19th century. Indeed, the United States did not receive its first significant wave of Jewish immigrants until 1830–60, when approximately 144,000 German Jews came to seek their fortune in the United States. Many of these newcomers established small businesses, and some transformed their initial holdings into retail empires. Within a generation, German Jews had become a prosperous group that had won the respect and acceptance of their Gentile (non-Jewish) compatriots.

By the end of the century, however, these respected citizens felt their great success threatened—not by events occurring in America but by developments taking place in Europe. In the 1880s a wave of anti-Semitic violence swept through Russia and eastern Poland — the countries containing the largest Jewish populations in Europe. Droves of persecuted Jews fled to America, not simply to better their economic prospects, as their German predecessors had, but to save their lives.

Between the 1880s and the 1920s, steamships brought 3.5 million eastern European Jews into New York Harbor, many of them arriving with empty pockets. Before long, this mass of immigrants had risen to become one of the most accomplished ethnic communities in America. Jewish Americans have sat on the Supreme Court, held distinguished professorships at the nation's best universities, and won every conceivable award in literature, the arts, and the sciences (including numerous Nobel Prizes). Jewish Americans have shaped the tastes of their neighbors through Hollywood films, in dramas and musicals that have dominated the Broadway stage, and in concert halls throughout America. They also had a mighty influence on the growth of investment banking and finance — hence, on the vitality of the economy.

This remarkable record has occasioned much debate among those seeking to explain it. One factor in the success of Jewish Americans, surely, has been education. Learning figures importantly in the Jewish tradition; the impoverished Jews of eastern Europe looked up to the scholars among them who devoted their lives to studying the Bible and the Talmud, a written code of Jewish law. For the Jews of western Europe, the tradition of intellectual rigor often translated into brilliantly innovative ideas. The economist Karl Marx, the physicist Albert Einstein, and the founder of pyschoanalysis, Sigmund Freud — three of the greatest thinkers of modern times — exemplify the ideal of the erudite, Continental Jew.

The majority of Jewish Americans are descendants of poor, uneducated refugees from eastern Europe who had no opportunity to excel outside the narrow confines of provincial Old World villages—or *shtetls*. But once immigrants from these deprived places reached America, their thirst for knowledge spilled into the secular realm. The result was an extraordinarily well educated ethnic community: Today some 80 percent of America's Jews have been to college, and half of those hold advanced degrees.

American Jews have similarly been driven by the desire to better their economic and social status. The eastern European Jews who immigrated to this country between 1881 and 1924 quickly reaped material rewards. The percentage of workers holding white-collar jobs (as opposed to blue-collar, or manual, jobs) easily surpasses the rate among the general population. And Jews account for a large number of the nation's physicians, lawyers, and professors.

Though the first generation of immigrant Jews prospered mainly by running small businesses, today Jewish Americans can be found in the boardrooms of the nation's most powerful corporations. This change was dramatized in 1973 when a Jewish executive, Irving S. Shapiro, assumed the position of chairman and chief executive officer at E. I. du Pont de Nemours and Company, one of the country's oldest and most prestigious companies.

New York's Educational Alliance library served immigrants eager to learn about life in America.

The United States has opened so many doors to Jews that it boasts more members of the group than any other nation—some 6 million. (North America's other Jews, those in Canada, number more than 300,000.) Israel, with about 3.3 million Jews, claims the second largest number, and third comes the Soviet Union, with a Jewish population of 2 million in 1987. In this year, more than half of America's Jews lived in the northeastern states, and about 33 percent resided in the New York metropolitan area. Numbers were growing also in the southern and western states; more than 500,000 Jews lived in metropolitan Los Angeles, for example. After New York, California and Florida had the highest Jewish populations. The 3 states in which Jews formed the highest *percentage* of the population were New York (10.8 pecent), New Jersey (5.7 percent), and Florida (5.2 percent).

A bride and groom take their vows beneath the khupe, *a traditional Jewish wedding canopy.*

Overall, Jews constitute less than three percent of the American population—a relatively small portion. A low birthrate has been cause for concern among Jews; so has intermarriage with Gentiles. For decades it has been predicted that intermarriage and assimilation might destroy Jewish culture in America, but so far the pessimists have been proved wrong. American Jews have retained a high degree of Jewish consciousness while remaining deeply committed Americans. In other times, in other countries, Jews have been accused of forming a separate bloc with more loyalty to the "Jewish nation" than to their home country. But aside from the jabs of a few bigots, that charge is not often seriously raised against American Jews.

Anti-Semites who question the loyalty of Jewish Americans or their "real" intentions in the United States err further in lumping together all Jews without taking into account the enormous diversity of American Judaism. Religious Jews generally fall into three groupings: Orthodox, Conservative, and Reform. Orthodox Jews, the most traditional, interpret the biblical Old Testament as the word of God and attempt to obey its strictures to the letter. Conservatives regard their religion as a dynamic one and feel that the Old Testament must be continually reinterpreted to meet the demands of changing times. Reform Judaism, shaped to a large extent by Jews in America, views the religion as a form of ethical monotheism (belief in a single god) whose meaning may differ for each individual believer. Reform Jews also reject some of the ancient traditions— such as dietary laws and services entirely in the Hebrew language—practiced by Orthodox and Conservative Jews.

Judaism is also more than a religion; it is a culture rooted in a remarkable and often tragic history. Even Jews who never step inside a synagogue or celebrate religious holidays often consider themselves Jews and are viewed as such by their neighbors. The thorny question of Jewish identity—who, exactly, is a Jew?—will continue to be debated for years to come. ❧

The candelabra on this carved Roman sarcophagus—from the 3rd or 4th century—identifies it as belonging to a Jew.

WHO ARE THE JEWS?

Are the Jews a religious or an ethnic group? According to Orthodox Jewish law a Jew is either the child of a Jewish mother or a convert to the Jewish religion. Many Jews, however, do not observe the religious dictates of Judaism, though they feel a connection to Jewish history. At the same time, Jews do not claim a unique ethnicity: They are Semites, but so are other peoples whose ancestry traces back to the Middle East and who are found from Morocco to the Persian Gulf. And Jewish populations exist in Africa, India, and the Orient.

Four thousand years ago the ancestors of modern-day Jews were known as Hebrews, a tribe whose dramatic and painful story anticipates the later history of the Jewish people. In the desert surrounding Canaan, the Hebrews lived as nomads, much like other tribes across the Middle East, and roamed a barren land that barely sustained them. Three Hebrew patriarchs—Abraham, his son Isaac, and his grandson Jacob—called the land of Canaan their home. Later, that region came to be known as Palestine, and after 1948 the same general area acquired yet another name, Israel.

The Dawn of Judaism

In about 1700 B.C. famine struck the Hebrews. They migrated from Canaan to Egypt, where they remained until about 1280 B.C., when the pharaoh Ramses II took advantage of their vulnerable status by enslaving them.

19

The story of Abraham and his son Isaac was depicted by the Florentine sculptor Lorenzo Ghiberti in his Gates of Paradise, *a set of bronze doors he created between 1403 and 1424.*

He called the refugees "strangers in a strange land," a phrase that has since come to summarize the Jews' beleaguered history. Because the laws of Egyptian society protected only property, the Hebrews could not escape servitude and saw little hope of ever regaining their freedom. Nevertheless, they recognized that as long as they remained under the pharaoh's thumb they must band together as a group to ensure their survival outside the ancient homeland.

In about 1225 B.C. there occurred the single most important event in the consolidation of Jewish identity: The prophet Moses organized the Hebrew slaves and led them out of Egypt. The biblical book Exodus describes this trek across the Red Sea into the Sinai Desert:

And Moses stretched out his hand over the sea; and the Lord caused the sea to go back by a strong east wind all that night, and made the sea dry land and the waters were divided.

And the children of Israel went into the midst of the sea upon the dry ground; and the waters were a wall unto them on their right hand, and on their left.

Their journey across the desert toward Canaan was an arduous one, but they were fortified at Mount Sinai, where Moses read the Ten Commandments from stone tablets said to have been sent down to earth by God himself. The Ten Commandments—or the Decalogue—exhorted the Jews to act in a manner governed by moral and ethical considerations: "Honor thy father and mother. . . . Thou shalt not kill. . . . Thou shalt not commit adultery. . . . Neither shalt thou bear false witness against thy neighbor. . . . " Believing that a divine voice had addressed them, the Hebrews abandoned polytheism (the worship of many spirits) and instead dedicated themselves to monotheism, the belief in a single, all-powerful deity. They called their god

Moses leads the Jews across the Red Sea in a 15th-century woodcut from a German Bible designed by Johannes Gutenberg, the father of modern printing.

Yahweh, the God of the Jews. Because God had singled them out to be his followers, the Hebrews came to consider themselves the "chosen people."

The Kingdom of Israel

The story of these roughly 800 years—from Abraham to enslavement to freedom under the leadership of Moses—is documented in the first five books of the biblical Old Testament: Genesis, Exodus, Leviticus, Numbers, and Deuteronomy, known collectively as the Torah, the linchpin of the Jewish faith.

After leaving Mount Sinai, ancient Jews reached the "Promised Land"—Palestine—and found safe haven there, living under the benign rule of the Judges, so-

Sephardic Jews have traditionally enclosed their Torahs in elaborate cases such as this one, made in Paris in 1860.

cially progressive leaders who even admitted a woman, Deborah, to their inner circle. Later, when the Jews installed a monarchy—in about 1000 B.C.—their second king, David, established Jerusalem as the capital city. But within a generation, Palestine was divided into two kingdoms, Israel to the north and Judah (from which the word *Jew* originates) to the south.

This division weakened the kingdoms and perhaps contributed to the subsequent downfall of Israel in the north: In 721 B.C. this kingdom fell first to the Assyrians and later to the Babylonians, who in 586 B.C. razed the Jews' house of worship, the First Temple, in Jerusalem. Their homeland occupied, the Jews of Israel faced the bitter prospect of wandering endlessly on its periphery.

The Jews' adversity only strengthened their faith in Yahweh, their commitment to live in accordance with the Torah, and their certainty that someday they would reclaim their rightful home. Their dreams materialized in 538 B.C. when the Persians invaded Israel and, after ousting the Babylonian forces there, allowed the Jews to return. Gladdened by this homecoming, they entered a period of spiritual revival, vowing an even stricter adherence to the Mosaic Code and replacing their demolished temple with a second one.

The Diaspora

Defeat came again, however, at the hands of the Romans, whose imperial ambitions had driven them east to Palestine. The Romans first maintained a small army near Jerusalem, then launched a full-scale invasion and forcibly entered the city, destroying the Second Temple in A.D. 70. In A.D. 135, the Romans officially outlawed Judaism and ordered the Jews to disperse throughout the Roman world.

This dispersal—or Diaspora—had two important conseqences. First, Jews directed their energies away from establishing a homeland and focused instead on scholarly aims, applying themselves to an intense study

Roman soldiers plunder Jerusalem's Second Temple in this relief from the Arch of Titus, erected in A.D. 81 to honor the Roman emperor who conquered the Jews.

of their holy books. Second, Judaic thought and culture spread to the far-flung corners of the Roman Empire—Europe, North Africa, and the Levant (the countries bordering the eastern part of the Mediterranean Sea).

Before long, Jews made up about one-tenth of the Roman Empire's population, and the notion of an isolated "Jewish race" vanished amid the growing numbers of Jews scattered across the map. In fact, even a few important Roman officials converted to Judaism despite the Roman injunction against the religion and despite the fact that the waning empire adopted Christianity as its official religion after A.D. 313.

From the distance of 1,900 years, it may look as though Jews practiced a uniform creed before the Roman invasion. But even as the majority recited prayers from the Torah in Jerusalem's temples, others offered resistance to the monotheistic call of the First Commandment, "Thou shalt have no other gods before me." Various sects, many standing in blatant opposition to the teachings of Judaism, sprang up under charismatic leaders. One such leader, Jesus Christ, expounded a philosophy based on many of the precepts of Judaic thought. His followers accepted him as the Messiah (in fact, the name *Jesus Christ* is a translation from classical Greek of *Joshua the Messiah*), and his teachings gained enormous influence.

Secure in the sanctuary of their homeland, Jews freely disagreed among themselves. But exile thrust them into alien lands with competing theologies, and their differences mended. Jews devoted themselves to the practice of Judaism with renewed fervor, and their beliefs took on a more uniform cast. Although thousands of miles separated Jews from Palestine, Judaism endured.

Across Europe

Dispersed throughout foreign, often hostile, lands, Jews faced anti-Semitism so extreme that it menaced their survival as a people. Many Christians blamed Jews for killing Jesus Christ, when in fact Jews and Romans

French Jews of the 12th century illustrated this edition of the Mishna, a codification of Jewish law included in the Talmud.

together—alarmed by Christ's growing power in Jerusalem—had conspired to end his life. Christians reacted by identifying Jews as the "Antichrist" and outlawing Judaism in parts of the Middle East and Europe, where many transplanted Jews had settled. In order to break the Jews' spirit, Europeans burned their synagogues and settlements during much of the first millennium A.D.

Yet somehow Judaism thrived. Generations of rabbis, scholars, and laymen studied the Torah meticulously, and the body of their commentary grew into the Talmud, a codification of Jewish law, encyclopedic in scope, set down in the 5th century and repeatedly refined and reinterpreted. In such centers of Jewish life as Mesopotamia, Spain, and (later) the Rhineland, experts on Jewish law guided other Jews on civic as well as spiritual matters.

As the years passed, Jews fanned out across North Africa and most of Europe. They did not again constitute a majority of any nation's population, as they had in Palestine, but they made their presence felt. In Spain, for example, where Jews flourished from the 9th through the 15th centuries, a Jewish literary revival took root and enriched the national culture. Spain's tolerance of Jews had no equal in medieval Europe. In other countries, virtually all power and wealth belonged to the aristocracy and to the Catholic church, leaving Jews without a voice. Moreover, laws denied Jews the right to own land and to enter most professions.

In the 10th and 11th centuries, trade and commerce began to grow in Europe. Merchants from cities in France and Italy journeyed all the way to the Orient to obtain silks and spices. These adventurous traders included Jews, whose dispersal provided them with an international network of potential business partners who spoke the same language and shared the same beliefs. This network seemed the perfect means for the Jews to establish an independent trade route, one that would enable them to compete in the marketplace.

But once again, Jews found their hands tied, this time by powerful Gentile merchants who barred Jews from trading. At this point, nearly every occupation was closed to them. In desperation, Jews flocked to one of the few open professions: finance. The mercantile economy of the late Middle Ages depended on money to grease the wheels of trade, but the Catholic church frowned on moneylending as a vice fit only for infidels. Naturally, no objection was raised when Jews stepped in to fill the role of banker.

Meanwhile, bigotry continued its march throughout Europe. Jews were banished from England in 1290, from France in 1394, and from Spain in 1492. During the 300-year reign of terror now known as the Spanish Inquisition, hundreds of thousands of Jews who refused to convert to Catholicism were burned alive, tortured, or locked in dungeons. In German territories, expulsion of the Jewish population followed a series of massacres. There, as in Spain, some Jews professed belief in Catholicism in order to save their lives; others actually converted; and many chose to die rather than renounce their faith. The Germans burned Jewish books and desecrated synagogues, acts that were repeated by the Nazis in the 20th century.

In the 15th and 16th centuries Poland alone provided a safe haven for Jews, especially for those driven eastward from Germany. Polish leaders took the radical step of introducing rights for Jews into the country's legal code and also protected their commercial activities. The Jews who entered Poland permanently became known as Ashkenazim, a name derived from the Hebrew word for Germany. By the 1900s, a majority of the Continent's Jewish population had migrated to Poland. This concentration in a single country eventually contributed to their downfall, however; during World War II, the German Nazis destroyed nearly half of Europe's Jewish population by rounding up those residing in Poland.

Generally, Jews of the 15th and 16th centuries fared better in countries with Islamic rulers than they did in Christian ones. Turkey, for instance, granted entry to many victims of the Diaspora. Later, during the Spanish Inquisition, the Turkish Ottoman Empire opened its doors to Sephardim—Jews from Spain—an acceptance that proved both a blessing and a curse. In Turkey, Jews gained more freedom than they had known in Europe. Yet as they intermingled with the Muslim majority, their religion became diluted with elements of Islamic mysticism.

Some responded to this unwanted influence by migrating back to Palestine and its growing Jewish population. Others went to northern Europe—especially Hamburg, Germany; London, England; and Amsterdam, Holland. These cities had become centers of Protestantism, a branch of Christianity opposed to Catholicism. In Protestant Europe, Jews could worship and conduct business as they chose, without the constant threat of persecution.

These cities gave rise to a new phenomenon, the Westernized Jew. Earlier European Jews had managed

A miniature from a 13th-century European Bible depicts King Solomon reading from the Torah.

Baron James de Rothschild (1792–1868), who made his home in France, often used his considerable influence with that country's government to aid fellow Jews at home and abroad.

to retain their faith because they were exposed to no rival religions and came into contact with other Jews. Now that they could move freely in society, Jews of northern Europe longed to participate in the wider secular world but were excluded from it by their own tradition and philosophy. Many felt torn between their devotion to Judaism and their desire to sample the pleasures of a cosmopolitan life.

A new era for the rights of Jews (as for many others) loomed in 1789, when the French Revolution introduced liberal values that traveled throughout the Continent. By the mid-19th century Jews had won political emancipation in most of western Europe, and in 1858 the first Jew gained a seat in England's Parliament. The new liberal climate fostered the advancement of numerous Jews, most notably the Rothschilds, a family of financiers. Other Jews became prominent artists, scientists, and statesmen, though such success entailed compromise—Britain's prime minister Benjamin Disraeli, for example, expediently converted to Christianity early in his life. As religious tolerance increased, it eroded the cultural and social boundaries that had always divided Jews and Gentiles. In many western European cities, ghettos vanished, their residents free to live wherever they pleased.

Progress marked Jewish life in France, England, Germany, and Holland, but the 4 million Jews of eastern Europe never enjoyed the rights of full citizenship. In 1880, nearly half of world Jewry was isolated inside the Pale of Settlement—an area of eastern Poland and western Russia to which all the Jews of the region had been consigned. These Jews usually lived in isolated and impoverished villages or shtetls. This insularity served the Jews well, however, first by spawning a vibrant Jewish culture and second by leaving Jews relatively free from direct intervention in their daily lives.

During the 18th century, Polish shtetls gave birth to the popular Orthodox movement practiced by the Hasidim (Hebrew for "pious ones"). Hasidic rabbis railed against the tradition of scholarship within Judaism. They argued that God wanted Jews to believe with their hearts—not their minds. The Hasidim practiced an emotional, almost ecstatic type of prayer that they believed would afford them direct connection with God. In order to distinguish themselves from the other Jews around them, Hasidic men adopted the style of dress of Polish noblemen; even today they wear long black coats. At its peak, Hasidism claimed followers among roughly half of Europe's Jews.

Although Hasidim and other Jews of eastern Europe remained sequestered within the Pale, their mere presence riled Gentile authorities. Also in 1648 marauding Cossacks—cavalrymen in the czar's army—killed 100,000 Jews, and similar butchery continued for the next 250 years. Continous waves of massacres—or *pogroms*—kept Jews in a state of constant terror. The killers justified their deeds first as a religious obligation (Jews, they argued, posed a threat to the mother church of Russia) and then as a racial one (Jews were not Slavs). This prolonged persecution, which climaxed in 1881 and again in 1904, drove millions of Jews to leave their "nation" for America between 1880 and 1920.

Oppression rekindled the Jews' desire for a homeland. One Jew in particular, Theodor Herzl, a Hungarian, argued that the only remedy for persecution was for Jews to establish an independent state in Palestine. Toward that end he organized a formal movement, called Zionism, and in 1896 published a highly influential pamphlet, *The Jewish State*. The following year, Herzl convened the first World Zionist Congress, in Basel, Switzerland. His efforts won much support, but a majority of the Jewish population found the prospect of a Jewish state hopelessly unrealistic: Palestine, after all, remained a part of the Turkish Ottoman Empire.

But for once fortune smiled on the Jews. The Turks were dislodged from Palestine after World War I, and the region's next occupiers, the British, found it so ungovernable that in 1947 they turned it over to the newly formed United Nations. American Jews were instrumental in promoting Zionism in the face of much resistance. After heated debate, the UN devised a compromise intended to satisfy the rival claims to Pal-

Today, Hasidic Jews in America generally live in urban neighborhoods such as Williamsburg in Brooklyn, New York.

estine put forth by Jews and Arabs, another group linked historically to the area. In 1948 Palestine was partitioned, and one of its separate states was granted to the Jews. Thus, nearly 2,000 years after Jews were expelled from the Promised Land and half a century after Herzl created the first Zionist Congress, the modern state of Israel was born.

Folkways

When Zionism first gained broad popularity, some eastern European Jews set out for the deserts of the Middle East to stake their claim in what would become Israel. Most, however, chose another route away from the hardships of the Pale and embarked for America, bringing with them traditional customs and a unique, hybrid language—Yiddish. Yiddish had its origins in the 10th century, when Jews from northern France settled along the Rhine River, absorbing German into their own vocabulary but writing it with the Hebrew alphabet. As the language evolved, about 70 percent of its words came directly from German, another 10 percent originated in Hebrew, and the rest filtered in from the native tongues of countries where Jews had settled. By World War II some 11 million Jews worldwide could understand Yiddish.

Most American-born Jews of the 20th century have abandoned the use of Yiddish, but recent concern that the language will disappear has sparked a modest Yiddish revival. Similarly, American Jews, and especially young adults, have shown increased interest in preserving the traditional Judaism practiced by grandparents and great-grandparents in the Old World.

Since their days in the deserts of Canaan, Jews have observed special dietary laws (called *kashrut*) set forth in the Old Testament. Their meat must come from animals that chew their cud and have cloven hooves (such as the cow and sheep), and their fish must have scales and fins. One passage from Leviticus lists some of the foods forbidden to them:

These also shall be unclean unto you among the
creeping things that creep upon the earth; the weasel,
and the mouse, and the tortoise after his kind,
And the ferret, and the chameleon, and the lizard, and
the snail, and the mole.

Such restrictions seem bizarre today, but in antiquity they probably served as a kind of public health code. Certain foods still not allowed under kashrut reflect the ancient concern with healthfulness: For example, pork, a known carrier of trichinosis, and shellfish, often tainted with hepatitis, both fall outside Jewish dietary law. Even foods that are *kosher*, or ritually correct, require special preparation under kashrut. Meats, unless boiled, must be cleansed with coarse salt and then soaked to remove all traces of blood. Meat and dairy products must be consumed separately and served with different sets of dishes and utensils.

Contemporary Jews do not universally observe the laws of kashrut, but the vast majority continue to celebrate the special holidays of Judaism. Many of these commemorate the cornerstones of Jewish history. During the yearly springtime feast of Passover, Jews reflect on the Exodus from Egypt and give thanks for their freedom. Most Christians probably do not realize that the Last Supper of Jesus Christ was in fact a *seder*, or Passover meal.

Theodor Herzl sits in the foreground of a group portrait photographed aboard a boat bound for Palestine.

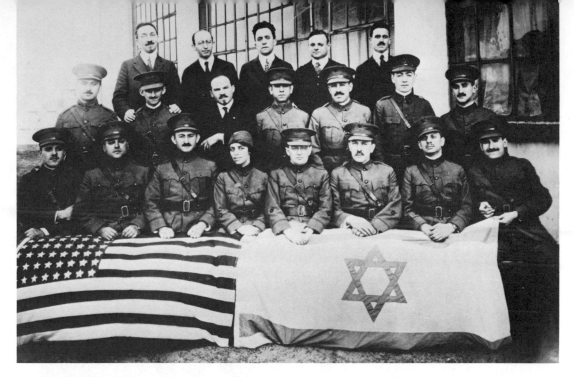

During December, the time of the winter solstice, Jews celebrate Hanukkah, the Festival of Lights, by giving gifts and lighting candles in a candelabra known as a *menorah*. The candles in the Hanukkah menorah represent eight miraculous days in which an oil lamp that contained enough fuel for only a single night, burned for seven more, illuminating Jerusalem's Second Temple.

The holiest time of year for Jews occurs in early autumn, the beginning of the Hebrew calendar year. Jewish "high holy days" commence with the New Year's celebration of Rosh Hashanah, an occasion marking the date on which—according to Jewish tradition—the world was created. Jews consider this a happy but solemn occasion, a time of self-scrutiny, when God passes annual judgment on his children. The contemplative mood of Rosh Hashanah intensifies during the most sacred day of the year, Yom Kippur (the Day of Atonement), observed by Jews with fasting and prayer. The ritual celebration of holidays such as Passover, Hanukkah, Rosh Hashanah, and Yom Kippur has kept Judaism alive throughout history and certainly sustained generations of Jews who immigrated to the alien lands of North America. ⤬

Many American Jews, such as the members of this volunteer medical corps stationed in Palestine, have supported the Zionist movement since its earliest days.

Canadian fur trader Albert N. Rose (far left) displays his wares at a trading post in Edmonton, Alberta.

WAVES OF IMMIGRATION

Nearly 2,000 Jews lived in the 13 colonies when the Declaration of Independence was signed in 1776. The history of Jewish Americans, however, began more than a century earlier, in September 1654. At the time, New York was still the Dutch colony of New Amsterdam, and Peter Stuyvesant was its governor. The city's latest arrivals included a group of 23 Jewish men, women, and children, refugees from Dutch Brazil. This land had recently been reconquered by its first colonists, the Portuguese, who refused to allow Jews in their territories.

The 23 Jews anticipated a warm reception in New Amsterdam, for its parent nation, Holland, had shown remarkable tolerance toward them. The Dutch capital, Amsterdam, housed a large Jewish community, one of the most vital in Europe. But in New Amsterdam the the Brazilian refugees got a chilly reception from Governor Stuyvesant, who had no fondness for religious dissenters. He wrote his employers, the Dutch West India Company, requesting permission to expel the newcomers in order that "the deceitful race,—such hateful enemies and blasphemers of the name of Christ,—be not allowed further to infect and trouble this new colony."

But Jews have always been good at organizing and lobbying. Back in Amsterdam, the Jewish community put pressure on the Dutch West India Company, which was responsible for much colonizing in North America. Jews argued that the New World still had plenty of room, that settlers were needed, and that more colonists meant increased revenue from trade and taxes. But it was probably an altogether different argument that hit a responsive nerve: "Your Honors should also please consider that many of the Jewish nation are principal shareholders in the Company." The company wrote back to New Amsterdam ordering Stuyvesant to let the Jews stay.

Over the next two centuries, the Jewish-American population grew slowly but steadily. These settlers faced prejudice similar to what they had known elsewhere; for example, restrictions sometimes limited their right to trade and to hold office. But men and women who showed they could work usually won their neighbors' respect. Besides, many of the colonists belonged to dissenting sects themselves and had suffered persecution. Thus, by the time of the Revolution the colonies had five Jewish congregations.

Uriah Philips Levy, the first Jewish American to obtain the rank of commodore in the United States Navy, fought in the War of 1812.

Jews showed their gratitude to their fellow colonists by taking an active part in the revolutionary war, both as soldiers and as suppliers for Washington's army. One of the Revolution's financiers was Haym Solomon, a Jew who first sold bonds and then expended all his own resources for the colonists' cause. And in 1790 a local newspaper printed correspondence between George Washington and the Jewish community of Newport, Rhode Island, the site of America's oldest temple, Touro Synagogue. The new president assured this enclave that the American government "gives to bigotry no sanction." Also, the Jews could rejoice when Article VI of the new Constitution ensured that "no religious test shall ever be required as a qualification to any office or public trust." The First Amendment proclaimed further that "Congress shall make no law respecting an establishment of religion, or prohibiting the free exercise thereof." To a population whose history consisted of almost uninterrupted persecution, these seemed magnificent guarantees. As a Philadelphia observer noted during a celebration for the new Constitution, "The rabbi of the Jews, locked in the arms of two ministers of the gospel, was a most delightful sight."

Despite America's tolerant laws, Jews hesitated to immigrate to the new country. During the first half century of the Republic, its Jewish population grew by only a few thousand. Jews held back in part because of the French Revolution. It occurred only a decade later than America's and offered Jews hope for a better life on a continent that, unlike North America, was familiar to them. Optimism grew in 1791, when France's National Assembly granted rights of citizenship to Jews.

But the outlook dimmed after the defeat of the French emperor Napoleon in the early 1800s. Throughout Europe, reactionary forces immediately attempted to turn back the clock. Jews lost most of the gains they had recently achieved, and a rash of anti-Semitic acts swept the Continent. For instance, the German kingdom of Bavaria (where Adolf Hitler launched his career a century later) oppressed Jews with burdensome taxes

In 1780, the United States issued this bank note to Haym Salomon, a Polish-born Jew who helped finance the American Revolution.

and with humiliating restrictions on the work they could perform and the places they could live. Authorities even imposed obstacles to marriage. The failure of a liberal uprising that took place in several German states (and swept across Europe) in 1848 also spurred tens of thousands of Germans, Jews among them, to emigrate.

The numbers tell the story. In 1830 about 6,000 Jews lived in the United States; most of them spoke English and had been born in the New World. Thirty years later, the Jewish-American population numbered 150,000, and the community largely spoke German. By 1880 the count had risen to 250,000, including the first wave of Yiddish-speaking Jews from eastern Europe. The leap from 6,000 to 250,000, though impressive, only hinted at what was to come. By 1920, the number of Jewish Americans reached *4 million*, the largest Jewish population in the world.

In 1880, an equivalent number (and half the world's Jews at the time) lived in the Russian Empire, restricted to the Pale of Settlement. Conditions there were miserable. Aside from the poverty of the shtetls and the outbreaks of government-sanctioned violence, Jews suffered from an unjust system of military conscription that forced Jewish men—sometimes boys as young as 12—to serve in the czar's army for as long as 25 years.

When Alexander II became czar in 1855, he initiated a number of mild reforms. But in 1881 he was assassinated by a terrorist bomb and the regime that succeeded stepped up hostilities against Jews. It passed anti-Semitic laws and virtually endorsed a series of pogroms—more than 200 in 1881 and 1882. The horror of the pogroms was described by the Russian revolutionary Leon Trotsky (himself a Jew, though by no means a religious one) in his account of a typical brute intoxicated by the thrill of violence:

> If he wants to, he can throw an old woman out of a third-floor window together with a grand piano, he can smash a chair against a baby's head . . . hammer a nail into a living human body. . . . He exterminates whole families, he pours petrol over a house, transforms it into a mass of flames, and if anyone attempts to escape, he finishes him off with a cudgel.

Faced with such terrorism, over a third of Russia's Jews departed in hordes—more than 90 percent of them bound for America, the land of promise. They were joined by Jews from the Austro-Hungarian Empire, where local conditions were often grim, and from Romania, where life was as bad as it was in the Pale.

An 1848 engraving depicts the struggle between German revolutionaries and the national parliament.

The trek to freedom was an ordeal. First of all, immigrants had to save enough money to make the journey—no easy task for those living in poverty. Next, they had to get to one of the European port cities, such as Hamburg or Amsterdam. The journey might involve stealing across a border; any draftable young Russian men discovered by the border authorities were collared and delivered to the army. Most of the immigrants had little or no urban experience. When they found themselves in big, unfamiliar cities, they were frightened and disoriented—perfect prey for cheaters and hucksters with reassuring smiles, ready to rob them of every penny.

The voyage across the ocean lasted several weeks. Most immigrants traveled in steerage, paying the cheapest rates for a place in the area under the deck, massed together amid nauseating squalor and stench. The steamship companies were stingy with food—religious Jews brought their own because the ships' food was not kosher—and even stingier with fresh water. Ventilation was terrible, and the air was thick with smells of excrement, tobacco, rotting food, sweat, and vomit—seasickness was a constant misery. Such discomforts especially distressed passengers uprooted from their lifelong homes, confused by contemptuous officials jab-

Immigrants en route to America gather on the steerage deck of the SS Pennland *in 1893.*

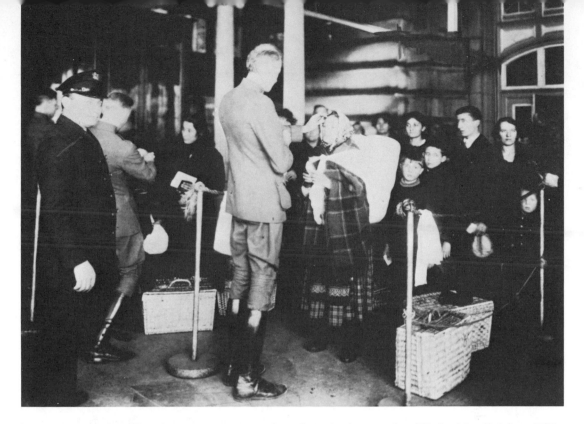

bering an unfamiliar language, uncertain of their futures, and above all, terrified that once they reached America they would not be admitted.

The first immigrants disembarked at Castle Garden, a huge, foreboding fortress off the southern tip of Manhattan. When the human flood became overwhelming, the processing center at nearby Ellis Island was opened, in 1892. At either site, the ordeal was terrifying. As one journalist wrote, "The day of the emigrants' arrival in New York was the nearest earthly likeness to the final Day of Judgement, when we have to prove our fitness to enter Heaven." The exhausted immigrants were pushed and pulled, shoved and shouted at. They were herded past a barrage of doctors who inspected them for tuberculosis and any number of other diseases or defects. Some were marked with chalk and placed in cagelike cells for further inspection; they might be kept on the island for a week or longer. After the examinations, officials drilled them with questions: Did they have money? A job lined up? Someone waiting to meet them?

A public health official on Ellis Island examines a woman's eyes for signs of disease, around 1900.

The trauma of Ellis Island was eased by organizations that American Jews had set up to help the immigrants. The best known and most successful was the Hebrew Immigrant Aid Society (HIAS), one of the first such organizations established by the eastern European Jews themselves rather than their German-Jewish predecessors. HIAS staff members acted as interpreters and mediators between government officials and the new arrivals. They gave the immigrants practical advice about life in the New World and protected them from sharpers and swindlers. They pressured the steamship companies to improve conditions in steerage; later on, they lobbied Congress against laws restricting immigration. Finally, the HIAS helped the new immigrants find jobs and even provided shelter for them.

From Ellis Island, most of the newcomers made their way into the slums and sweatshops of New York or other large American cities. The trip was over, and the days that ensued were hard, but hardship was something Jews had known for centuries. The flood from eastern Europe continued to increase as the new immigrants made a life for themselves and then sent for their families. At the turn of the century the Jewish community in the United States had grown to about 1 million. By 1910 it exceeded 2 million; by 1914 it had reached nearly 3 million; 10 years after that the number was approximately 4 million.

World War I brought immigration to a temporary halt, though it picked up again, briefly, after the war's end. But by the 1920s, America's hospitality was waning. In the aftermath of the war, the country adopted a policy of isolationism premised, in part, on widespread suspicion of foreigners. Anti-Semitism spread alarmingly (though not as alarmingly as it did in Europe). Moreover, the country's goals had changed. In the 19th century, when the country was expanding, immigrants were needed—for railroad building, factory work, and other industrial jobs. By the 1920s, the need had been quenched, and Congress passed laws cutting back on immigration in 1921, 1924, and 1927. After that, the flood dwindled to a trickle.

It picked up force again in the mid-1930s, when Jewish refugees from Hitler's Germany began arriving. These men and women came from backgrounds that differed markedly from those of the poor, unskilled eastern European immigrants of the previous half century. Most German refugees could afford to flee, and three-quarters of them were past the age of 40. They included lawyers, doctors, and merchants as well as brilliant scientists (including Albert Einstein), psychologists, scholars, writers, and artists. The 150,000 who came between 1935 and 1941 composed a large enough community for Manhattan's West Side—where most of the émigrés lived—to be nicknamed "the Fourth Reich."

But World War II led to one of the sadder chapters in Jewish immigration. Despite the tragic situation the Nazis had created in Europe, the United States Congress stubbornly refused to relax immigration quotas,

In 1889, Hester Street was home to thousands of Jewish immigrants on New York City's Lower East Side.

On October 1, 1940, the German physicist Albert Einstein was sworn in as a United States citizen, along with his daughter Margot (right) and his assistant, Helen Dukas.

and the State Department put up one obstacle after another for anyone seeking residence here. Jewish leaders appealed to President Franklin Delano Roosevelt to pressure Great Britain into letting more refugees into Palestine (present-day Israel, then under British control). But the U.S. government did very little. It even refused to bomb the gas chambers at Auschwitz—an act that might have saved thousands of Jewish lives—because it regarded such activity as a diversion from its main business: winning the war.

In recent decades, Jewish newcomers to America have arrived mainly from three countries: Iran, Israel, and the Soviet Union. In 1979, the shah of Iran was overthrown. The new Islamic fundamentalist government, under the leadership of the Ayatollah Ruhollah Khomeini, imprisoned or executed many members of the small Jewish population. Most of the rest eventually fled, including many who reached this country. America has also received a steady stream of immigrants from Israel. Some of these men and women found conditions too harsh in the Jewish state; others disliked living under the constant threat of war. Some simply viewed the United States the way Jews have for the last two centuries: as the land of opportunity.

The Soviet Union, with its roughly 2 million Jews, has the third-largest Jewish population in the world today, after the United States and Israel. But anti-Semitism there has never died out. The Soviet government has made life hard for Jews and has also made it hard for them to emigrate. Nevertheless—owing in part, no doubt, to pressure from the American government and in turn, from American Jews—more than a quarter of a million Russian Jews have been allowed to leave over the last couple of decades, and many have made their way to the United States.

Canadian Jews

In some aspects—most notably in its immigration history—the story of the Jews in Canada parallels that of Jews in the United States; but Judaism in Canada has developed its own distinct history. The date marking the first Jewish settlement there can be fixed precisely: 1759, the same year the British conquered the colony of New France. Until then, Jews had been barred by the French from France's North American territory in what is now Canada. Canadian Jews responded gratefully to British tolerance, repaying the favor with unwavering loyalty to the redcoats during the American Revolution in 1776. Later, during the War of 1812, Canadian Jews again supported the British against the Americans, despite strong family ties to Jews living in the new Republic.

Throughout the 19th century the British continued their tolerant treatment of Canadian Jews. In 1832 Jews received full civil rights, a privilege not yet enjoyed by Jews in the mother country of England. By 1867, when the provinces of Ontario, Quebec, New Brunswick, and Nova Scotia banded together to form the Dominion of Canada, about a thousand Jews lived in Canada, mainly in Montreal, Quebec City, Kingston, Toronto, and Hamilton. Most of these settlers traced their origins to western and central Europe.

The tidal wave of eastern European immigration that dramatically changed the face of Jewry in the United States also swept across Canada. By 1881 about 2,400 Jews had migrated there; by 1891 the figure had risen to 6,400; and by 1921, Canada's Jewish population had swelled to more than 126,000. Most immigrants made their new homes in Montreal and Toronto, gathering in dense, close-knit ghettos, as they did in so many cities in the United States.

Unlike their U.S. counterparts, however, Canadian Jews quickly moved westward—by 1920 the city of Winnipeg in the prairie province of Manitoba had the third-largest Jewish population in the country. Canada could also claim its share of Jewish farmers. The earliest eastern European immigrants had shown little talent for working the land, but with the help of the Jewish Colonization Association, Jews established farms in the provinces of Manitoba, Saskatchewan, Alberta, and, after World War I, in Ontario.

During World War II, Canada responded to the plight of European Jews with an indifference equal to America's. Canada remained all but closed to refugees: Between 1933 and 1945, fewer than 5,000 Jews were admitted, and after the holocaust Canada found room for only 8,000 additional survivors. When asked how many Jews would be allowed into Canada after the war, one Canadian official told a group of journalists: "None is too many." For the first time since it had officially accepted Jews, Canada seemed to be swayed by the anti-Semitism endemic in Europe. And alarmed Jewish citizens noticed an increased hostility in their countrymen.

Canadian Jews were relieved when this sudden malice receded at the war's end, and Jewish immigration

During the 1970s, the Brooklyn, New York, neighborhood of Brighton Beach was revitalized by an influx of Jewish refugees from the Soviet Union.

picked up shortly thereafter. After the failure of the 1956 anticommunist uprising in Hungary, Canada accepted thousands of Hungarian refugees, including 4,500 Jews. The later part of the decade saw the beginnings of an influx of French-speaking Jews from Morocco and other North African countries; these immigrants found a congenial welcome in French-speaking Quebec. In recent years, Canada has become home to Jewish refugees from the Soviet Union, who today number among the nation's more than 300,000 Jews—the sixth-largest Jewish population in the world.

LIFE IN AMERICA

For centuries, anti-Semitic laws in Europe had barred Jews from nearly every profession except commerce. They were prohibited from owning land—the principal source of wealth in agrarian society—and restricted also from becoming artisans because the medieval craft guilds denied them membership. Through necessity, Jews took on the roles of merchant and moneylender. These vocations also sustained them in America. As a 1738 observer in Georgia noted of the German-Jewish immigrants there, "They have no other profession besides farming or dealing in small trade. The latter comes easier to them than the former."

Although most Americans tilled the "fruited plains" to make their living, Jewish-American farmers were a rare sight in the 18th century. In the next two centuries many Jews tried vainly to sct up agricultural communities in the United States, but the majority failed dismally. Not until recently—when Israelis developed the cooperative farms known as *kibbutzim* and performed miracles of irrigation in the Middle Eastern desert—did Jews show any aptitude for working the land.

But they did have a knack for commerce. Long before the American Revolution, Jewish merchants had established successful stores in New York, Newport, Savannah, Philadelphia, and Charleston. Soon the commercial ties between Jews were strengthened by family

Many 19th-century German immigrants peddled household goods across America, traveling either by foot or with a horse and wagon.

alliances as the sons and daughters of wealthy merchants married one another. Such unions benefited immigrant Jews not only economically but also culturally, helping Jewish families retain their identity. In a land where the Jewish population was small—and where intermingling with Gentiles was unavoidable—Jews worried that their people would eventually disappear into the American melting pot.

The challenge of maintaining Jewish identity was most pronounced in small towns. Many early immigrants, eager to fit into American society, grew lax about such fundamental religious duties as keeping kosher households and observing the Jewish Sabbath, which falls on Saturday. In 1791, a woman in Petersburg, Virginia, wrote to her parents in Germany:

> I know quite well you will not want me to bring up my children like Gentiles. Here they cannot become anything else. Jewishness is pushed aside. . . . On the Sabbath all the Jewish shops are open; and they do business on that day as they do throughout the week.

Although this woman enjoyed small-town life in the United States—"You cannot know what a wonderful country this is for the common man"—she decided she must move to a city.

Jews from Germany

Beginning in 1830, anxieties about assimilation waned as German-Jewish immigrants flowed into the United States. Families from Germany typically migrated in several stages: a single family member, usually a son, came to America and saved sufficient earnings to bring over first one relative, then another. Most of these young immigrants took up peddling and supplied an expanding America with a host of sorely needed goods. As a rising number of Americans left the East Coast and ventured into wilderness territory they left behind the luxury of stores, usually shopping in town only once or twice a year. Thus, the peddler's cart was always a welcome sight. For their part, immigrants gravitated

In about 1890, employees pose in front of S. Lazarus & Company—a Columbus, Ohio, department store founded by Jewish Americans.

toward peddling because they could purchase their first bundle of goods on credit. Their packs, often weighing as much as 120 pounds, seemed backbreaking. "The walking of from ten to twenty miles per day I did not relish," one recalled dryly. Another noted in his journal:

> It is hard, very hard indeed, to make a living this way.
> Sweat runs down my body in great drops and my
> back seems to be breaking, but I cannot stop. . . .
> Each day I must ask and importune some farmer's wife
> to buy my wares, a few pennies' worth. Accursed
> desire for money, it is you that has driven the Bavarian
> immigrants to this wretched kind of trade!

German Jews quickly won a place in the American economy. The formula "from pack-on-back to store to department store" seems an exaggeration, but it accurately described the rapid climb many German-Jewish immigrants made up the financial ladder. And some farsighted entrepreneurs used their peddler's packs to lay the groundwork for businesses that grew into retail empires. Macy's and Gimbels in New York; F. & R. Lazarus in Columbus, Ohio; Filene's in Boston; Thalhimer Bros. in Richmond; Meier & Frank in Portland, Oregon—all had Jewish founders. Estée Lauder and Helena Rubinstein, in cosmetics, were two successful Jewish women who started out small, as was Lena (Lane) Bryant in fashion. Jews also moved successfully into meat packing, investment banking, and clothing manufacture.

The best-known clothing manufacturer was Levi Strauss, a Bavarian Jew who immigrated to this country in 1848, at the age of 17. In New York, he paid his dues as a peddler before accumulating enough capital to head for San Francisco. According to legend, he met a gold prospector there who glanced at the heavy fabric Strauss had brought with him and remarked, "You should have brought pants"—apparently mining was

By 1870, Levi Strauss had established himself as a successful merchant of ready-to-wear clothing.

rough on that particular item of clothing. The actual story is more complicated. A shrewd merchant, Strauss had already built up a flourishing San Francisco dry-goods business by 1872, when he received a letter from a Russian Jewish tailor living in Reno, Nevada, who had designed some heavy trousers from denim he had purchased from Levi Strauss & Co.: "The secret of them Pents is the Rivits that I put in those Pockets and I found the demand so large that I cannot make them up fast enough." Strauss must have been impressed,

A German-Jewish New Year's card from 1910 depicts an elegant holiday dinner.

because he decided to form a partnership with the tailor, procuring a patent to make "Levi's." Today Levi Strauss & Co. is a major manufacturing corporation, still centered in San Francisco and directed by Levi Strauss's heirs.

Other Jewish peddlers made their way to Cincinnati via Ohio River trade routes and built bustling shopping districts. These peddlers also erected garment factories—a natural extension of their retail businesses—and turned Cincinnati into a major center of clothing manufacture. This industry spawned a large, wealthy Jewish community, which founded the first American seminary for rabbinical training, Hebrew Union College.

A New Type of Immigrant

By 1880, Jewish Americans could feel extremely satisfied. They had achieved economic success; they had merged easily into American society; they had won the respect of their Gentile neighbors. But the situation suddenly changed. From 1880 to the mid-1920s, heavy waves of immigration swelled the country's Jewish population from 250,000 to more than 4 million.

The assimilated German Jews gazed uneasily on the mass migration. They had worked hard to combat the old Jewish stereotypes and to gain acceptance. Would all their progress be negated by invading hordes of eastern European paupers who appeared peculiar to American eyes, practiced Orthodox Judaism (in contrast to the more worldly Reform Judaism of the Germans), and seemed bumpkins hopelessly unprepared for America's big cities? Critical though they tended to be, some German Jews went to great lengths to ease the lives of the newcomers. They fought federal legislation that would have restricted immigration, and many Jewish philanthropic organizations got their start when German Jews reached out to help impoverished Russian Jews by establishing schools, libraries, and hospitals.

In New York, the "downtown" east Europeans on Manhattan's Lower East Side and the "uptown" Germans on the Upper West Side carried on a stormy relationship for decades; one uptown paper, finding the downtowners "slovenly in dress, loud in manners, and vulgar in discourse," declared that they had to "be

An eastern European immigrant prepares for the Sabbath in a coal cellar on Ludlow Street on the Lower East Side of New York City.

Americanized in spite of themselves, in the mode prescribed by their friends and benefactors." But however often and however deeply they offended one another, the two groups felt utterly bound by their Jewishness.

Urban Life

Unlike their German predecessors, who had spread west all the way to California, the eastern European migrants crowded together in the slums of major eastern and midwestern cities: Chicago, Philadelphia, Cleveland, St. Louis, Baltimore, Boston, and of course, New York. By 1910 there were more than half a million Jews squeezed into a 1½-square-mile patch on New York's Lower East Side. Conditions in the slums were deplorable: filthy, smelly, and above all, overcrowded. The apartments were cramped and dark. One contemporary report described a typical tenement flat:

> The parents occupy a small bedroom together with
> two, three or even four of the younger children. In the
> kitchen, on cots and on the floor, are the older children;
> in the front room two or more (in rare cases as many
> as five) lodgers sleep on the lounge, on the floor, and on
> cots, and in the fourth bedroom two lodgers . . .

Working conditions were even more appalling. Some of the new immigrants followed the example of the German Jews and became peddlers, lugging their packs door-to-door to earn a few pennies and a lot of derision. (The Jewish peddler seems to have been a favorite target of Irish-American boys with ripe fruit.)

Most of the new arrivals became fodder for the growing garment industry, centered at the time in squalid tenement quarters that came to be called "sweatshops." Many immigrants found jobs in the sweatshops because they had gained experience as tailors in the old country. Those unable to sew were hired as unskilled workers, operating the new machinery used

increasingly in the business. Immigrants also favored the clothing industry because it was owned, in large part, by other Jews. Eastern Europeans with memories of pogroms fresh in their minds welcomed the prospect of Jewish bosses, who at least shared their religion.

But a common heritage did not prevent bosses from mistreating sweatshop workers. Laborers earned next to nothing, and as a sympathetic observer sarcastically reported: "They work no longer than to nine o'clock at night, from daybreak." Hot, grimy, and crowded, the shops pushed exhausted workers to the limits of human tolerance, but a majority of immigrants felt they had to accept work on whatever terms it was offered. Garment

Jews do garment work in a New York City tenement in 1889.

In 1868 German Jews in New York dedicated Temple Emanu-El, a Reform synagogue whose grand scale reflected the community's wealth and power.

work was cyclical, and during the "slow season" jobs were scarce and competition for them fierce.

Like all immigrants, Jews scrimped, saved, and dreamed of a better life. A Chicago inspector reported:

A very large number speculate on the notion of opening, in course of time, a shop for themselves or going into business of some kind, or educating themselves out of the condition of the working classes. A large part of the tolerance of low wages, long hours of work, and unsanitary condition of the shops, that is, of the tragedy of economic servitude, of poverty, and of suffering, is to be ascribed to this state of mind.

The immigrants did not hope in vain. Within a few generations, many of their descendants would be living in comfort they themselves could scarcely imagine. Although some regarded American materialism as a spiritual trap, most immigrants struggled to better their plight. Grueling hours at work never deterred them from educating themselves in the ways, and especially the language, of the new country. An 1898 report in the *Atlantic Monthly* noted:

> Surely nothing can be more inspiring to the public-spirited citizen, nothing worthier of the interest of the student of immigration, than the sight of a gray-haired tailor, a patriarch in appearance, coming, after a hard day's work at a sweat-shop, to spell "cat, mat, rat," and to grapple with the difficulties of "th" and "w."

Immigrants in urban slums experienced every imaginable discomfort—hunger, sleeplessness, illness, and stifling quarters—but tried not to let these hardships wear at the fabric of domestic life. For generations, shtetl families had clung together through thick and thin, finding stability in well-defined roles. Jewish custom dictated that women reigned over the household and men supervised religious duties and wage earning. In the New World, the sexes divided labor in much the same fashion: Daughters might work in the sweatshops alongside sons until the demands of married life summoned them back to the home, where they sometimes labored at paid needlework to help support the family. Household activity often revolved around the kitchen. By day it harbored the cooking and washing, and by night it turned into a parlor, thus saving families the expense of heating the other rooms.

New Communities

Because New World Jewish society no longer revolved around shtetl life, immigrants had to improvise new communities. One organization important to them was the *landsmanshaft*, a club whose members came from the same shtetl or city in the old country. Most of the landsmanshaft formed between 1903 and 1909; at the height of their popularity, several thousand existed in America's cities, especially New York. Besides giving alienated immigrants a sense of belonging, these societies performed useful services: making burial arrangements and providing insurance, illness benefits, and low-cost loans. Landsmanshaft from the same area— Poland, Romania, or Galicia—might band together to support large charitable projects, such as hospitals or old-age homes. But the clubs were primarily social. The era of the landsmanshaft was short-lived (though by 1938 they still claimed three-quarters of a million members across the country); the members' native-born children, at home in America, rarely required the kind of support furnished by the clubs.

Jews also found companionship and comfort at the *shul*, the Orthodox synagogue. The German immigrants' brand of Judaism, Reform, had never appealed to the eastern European immigrants. For them traditional Orthodoxy supplied more than a mode of worship, it gave them a way of life, detailing rules and regulations for every imaginable circumstance. Not surprisingly, as the shtetl gave way to the big-city slum, the shtetl religion, Orthodox Judaism, became harder to practice. For example, Orthodox Jews consider Sabbath observance a sacred duty, but sometimes when the Sabbath arrived, they found it impossible to sacrifice a day's wages, particularly when their children were hungry. Such dilemmas began to undermine their religious practices.

Religious custom changed most drastically perhaps for those New World Jews who adopted Reform Judaism. A response to the strictness of Orthodoxy, the Reform movement began in the early 19th century and was transplanted to the American Midwest by German Jews, beginning in the 1840s. The leading reformer of this era, Isaac Mayer Wise (1819–1900), founded Hebrew Union College in Cincinnati, the city where he served as a rabbi for 35 years. Also an author, Wise

wrote novels, plays, essays, memoirs, and perhaps most important, a revised prayer book, which included an English or German translation of the Hebrew on each facing page. Through this book, *Minhag America* (*The American Rite*), English was introduced in the services.

The Reform cause Wise championed soon spread, catching on because it allowed for easier accommodation of new scientific ideas (including Darwin's theories of evolution) and for a revision of Jewish theology and ritual more in tune with life in America. Some outward restrictions in Jewish law were relaxed, for instance dietary laws that proved impractical in a frontier setting.

Jewish settlers in Montana pose with their rabbi, Samuel Schulman (third from left, bottom row), in a photograph taken ca. 1890.

The reform movement did not immediately find favor among newer immigrants, especially those from eastern Europe, but in Wise's opinion reform would come as the nation progressed. Followers of American Reform Judaism succeeded in maintaining most of their Old World beliefs and also in bringing those ancient beliefs in line with the evolving ideas of a growing country. Two innovations particularly applauded by Wise were the use of family pews in the synagogue (previously, members had been segregated by sex) and the inclusion of women in the choir.

As the observance of religion changed, so, too, did the role of the religious leader, the rabbi. Traditionally, the shtetl rabbi acted as a combination of teacher, community leader, and judge. In the United States, the power of this traditional figure of authority diminished greatly because law was interpreted by civil courts. In fact, rabbis in the United States relinquished all their customary duties but one: conducting religious sevices. This loss of status accompanied a general shifting of values within the Jewish community in the New World. Shul attendance dropped dramatically. Still, thousands who lost the habit of everyday religious observance remained believers, and on the High Holy Days—Rosh Hashanah and Yom Kippur—Jews continued to fill the Orthodox shuls. These places of worship exerted a nostalgic, emotional pull. They were links to the old country, and they seemed much warmer and more welcoming than their cosmopolitan stepchild, Reform temples.

The Jewish Press

Some Jewish interests fell by the wayside in America, but others found new life. Few other immigrant groups have taken to journalism as enthusiastically as the Jews. Since the earliest days of the Republic, the Jews have published, written for, and been avid readers of the nation's newspapers. By 1823, Jewish colonists could claim their own newspaper, called, simply, *The Jew*, published in New York City. Although it lasted only

Editor Abraham Cahan advocated socialism in the pages of his newspaper, the Jewish Daily Forward.

two years, it had many successors. Throughout the latter half of the 19th century, the Jewish press bloomed in the United States, finally producing as many as 90 journals, including *The Israelite* in Cincinnati, *The Jewish Voice* in St. Louis, *The Jewish Spectator* in Memphis, and *The Occident* in Chicago; Philadelphia, Cleveland, and Montreal all had their own dailies. Between 1900 and 1920 hundreds more appeared. These papers ran news and feature articles as well as poetry and fiction by leading Yiddish writers. The foremost Orthodox paper, the *Yidisher Tageblatt*, beat a drum for traditional values. There was also the moderately liberal, moderately Zionist *Tog*.

Addie Kahn (née Wolff), wife of banker Otto Kahn, epitomized the gentility of New York's German-Jewish elite.

The most popular Yiddish daily, the socialist *Jewish Daily Forward*, had 200,000 regular readers at its peak. Its editor, Abraham Cahan, became one of the most influential men in the immigrant community. A Lithuanian Jew, he immigrated to America in 1882 at the age of 22 and soon enlisted in left-wing causes, gaining a reputation as a lively speaker. Cahan achieved even greater renown as a writer, as gifted in English as in Yiddish. His 1917 novel *The Rise of David Levinsky* remains a classic of immigrant life.

But it was as editor of the *Forward* that Cahan wielded the most influence. He believed that the best way to bring socialist thought to a wide, largely unsophisticated audience was not through a party organ but through a popular newspaper. The *Forward* ran plenty of news and commentary, but it also packed in scandal, crime, and human-interest stories. Its most popular fea-

(continued on page 73)

A NEW YORK MONTAGE

(Overleaf) Skyscrapers frame a menorah placed in midtown Manhattan by Lubavitch Jews, members of the Hasidic community.

Traditional Jewish holidays celebrate a history of survival against overwhelming odds. The Hanukkah menorah (above)—a nine-branched candelabra lit during the Festival of Lights—symbolizes an oil lamp that held enough fuel for a single night but miraculously burned for eight. At the Passover seder (right), Jews read from the Haggadah, which describes their ancestors' exodus from Egypt in the 13th century B.C.

Modern Judaism divides into three distinct categories. At Orthodox synagogues (above, left) women must gather separately behind a screen to read from the Torah, whereas Reform Judaism—born in the 19th century— allows men and women to worship together and includes innovations such as the confirmation ceremony (below, left). Conservative Judaism—a compromise between the old and the new—now accepts women into the rabbinate. Above, two rabbinical students at the Jewish Theological Seminary meet with their chancellor.

A third of America's 6 million Jews live in New York, where their culture remains a vital force: A Brooklyn pizzeria offers kosher fare; a parade up Manhattan's Fifth Avenue honors the nation of Israel; and couples dance in the Catskills, a mountain resort area long favored by Jewish Americans.

71

The world of finance includes many venerable firms founded by Jewish Americans. Top executives convene for an informal photo session at Lehman Brothers, a leading Wall Street brokerage that in 1984 merged with Shearson Hayden, Stone Inc. to form Shearson Lehman Brothers, now a subsidiary of American Express.

(continued from page 64)

ture was an advice column called "A Bintel Brief" ("A Bundle of Letters"), a kind of Yiddish "Dear Abby."

The *Forward* strongly supported the Jewish labor unions, and it contributed generously to strike funds and other left-wing causes. But, more than a socialist paper, it was a *Jewish* paper—the largest Yiddish daily in the world—offering not only political but practical guidance. The *Forward* linked the immigrant community to mysterious America—explaining, for example, the ins and outs of baseball or insisting, over and over, on the importance of learning English. Cahan died in 1951, but The *Forward* is still being published.

Bankers and Financiers

In the last third of the 19th century and the early years of the 20th, the American economy grew enormously, and workers and owners from many nations participated in the industrial and financial boom. Jewish Americans played a major role in this growth, chiefly through the big New York merchant banks they had founded or built. At first, most of these businessmen were German by birth—Seligman, Loeb, Kuhn, Warburg, Schiff, Guggenheim—but as the 20th century wore on, Jews from eastern Europe also entered what the Germans had once called "our crowd." The Jewish "crowd" arose because a man such as Jacob Schiff, who acted as J. P. Morgan's banker in some of that magnate's early railroad deals, was excluded from the social world inhabited by his client.

Today, many of Wall Street's biggest brokerages and investment banks still bear the names of Jewish-American founders: Shearson Lehman Brothers, Salomon Brothers, Goldman Sachs & Co. These firms are staffed by descendants of the early millionaires and also by the sons and daughters of poor immigrants who made good in subsequent generations. The early banking fortunes have benefited the public as well, with funding for museums, hospitals, schools, and dozens of other foundations and charities. ⮰

In a 1909 demonstration, two young socialists carry banners bearing identical slogans in Yiddish and in English.

ORGANIZING, ACTIVITISM, POLITICS

The Jewish passion for political freedom can be traced back to ancient times, when Moses revealed the Decalogue at Mount Sinai. According to one interpretation, this founding doctrine of Judaism espouses the idea, revolutionary for its time, that "man is more than property; even to his master he gives only his service. His person is free."

Not all American Jews sided with the cause of personal liberty, however. In the 19th century, many Jews in the Southern states joined the proslavery ranks. Some rabbis actually owned slaves and gave sermons that cited Scripture in defense of the "peculiar institution." A proslavery senator from Louisiana and one of the most prominent Jews of the age, Judah P. Benjamin, earned the label "an Israelite with Egyptian principles." Benjamin belonged to the Confederacy leadership and was appointed its secretary of state during the Civil War.

But the great majority of American Jews lived in the North and opposed slavery. Many became abolitionists, social activists who demanded the compulsory emancipation of black slaves. As civil war loomed in 1860, they joined the ranks of the Republican party, backing its presidential candidate, Abraham Lincoln. After the war's end, Northern Jews continued to support the Republicans, though some objected when the commander of the victorious Union forces, General Ulysses S. Grant, reputedly an anti-Semite, won the nomination of Lincoln's party in the 1872 presidential election.

Jewish Proletarians

Jewish Americans did not become identified with political activism until, the 1880s, when the mass of refugees arrived from eastern Europe. These immigrants included some witnesses of the wave of revolutions that in 1848–49 swept across Italy, France, Austria, Hungary, Poland, and Germany. Even those born after the ferment subsided shared a memory of it, and in the United States this memory resurfaced in the passionate guise of social reform. Generations of Jewish Americans flung themselves into the thick of the labor frays that have helped define the nation's political life during the last 100 years.

Many of the Jews who landed on our shores in the 1880s settled in New York City and immediately sought employment. Thousands found jobs in the sweatshops, toiling at sewing machines for 12 to 15 hours a day. Employers often required them to work straight through the week, sometimes hanging signs that read, "If you don't come in on Sunday, don't come in on Monday."

Immigrants endured this treatment because they had a clear-cut goal—saving enough money to pay their family's passage from Europe. But the daily grind of the sweatshop routine became too much even for self-denying immigrants, and many rebelled, blaming their suffering on an economic system that rewarded only competition and financial gain. The workplace would be more humane, they argued, if businesses were taken from the hands of individual owners and placed under the joint stewardship of labor and management.

This proposal grew out of a new political ideology, socialism, that developed in Europe in the mid-19th century. Socialist theory responded to a drastic change in the Continent's economy, as the industrial revolution drew millions of farmers away from the land and into the bleak factories springing up in Europe's cities. In London, Paris, Berlin—and a host of smaller urban centers—men, women, and children suffered the drudgery of killing hours, the humiliation of measly wages, and the cruel awareness that the profits of their labor fattened the purses of factory owners.

Many social critics and social philosophers suggested ways of eliminating these inequities. The most brilliant and radical was the German-Jewish thinker Karl Marx, who in 1848 collaborated with his compatriot, Friedrich Engels, on the *Communist Manifesto*. This tract called not only for factories but entire nations to be run cooperatively under the leadership of the working class; this form of government is called communism.

A New York City sweatshop in the early 1900s.

Jewish-American radicals versed in Marxist ideology applied its prescriptions to their own plight. Leaders arose from the ranks of sweatshop laborers and organized their co-workers into unions—a task that seemed hopeless at first because so many obstacles stood in their way, including the reluctance of the garment workers. Many had families to support and realized that participating in a strike meant being fired—or worse, being blacklisted throughout the entire industry as a trouble-maker. And in an era that had no unemployment compensation, losing a job could mean starvation.

But wretched conditions in the sweatshops finally outweighed the security of steady work, and in the 1880s and 1890s laborers organized small work-stoppage strikes. Often they won concessions from employers, though once a walkout concluded, the strikers again settled into the old routine rather than try to create a permament industry-wide union. A core of labor leaders kept the union movement alive, however, and

Revolutionary philosopher Karl Marx began his masterwork Das Kapital, *an analysis of capitalist economics, in 1867.*

Alexander Berkman, a German anarchist, addresses a socialist crowd in New York City's Union Square on May Day, 1908.

gradually convinced their fellow workers that they must band together if they hoped to gain power. By the late 19th century, unions and federations of unions had begun forming in cities across America. In New York, the United Hebrew Trades was organized in 1888; within three years, 40 unions were associated with it. Chicago workers laid the foundation for a labor federation with the Jewish Workers Educational Society; in Philadelphia, it was the Jewish Federation of Labor.

Socialists considered themselves part of an international workers' movement. (Their slogan, taken from the *Communist Manifesto*, was "Workers of the world, unite!") They believed that poor workers should identify first and foremost with other members of their class rather than with those of the same nationality or religion. In their view a garment worker in New York had far more in common with a British coal miner than with middle-class American Jews.

Such strong class identification sometimes put activists at odds with Judaism, even though many were either immigrants or first-generation Americans raised

Emma Goldman speaks out in support of birth control in Union Square, 1910.

in the tradition of religious Orthodoxy. To an extent, Jewish-American socialists rebelled against their own backgrounds as well as against the evils of "capitalist exploitation." Some shocked fellow Jews by committing intentional sacrilege, even organizing parties on Yom Kippur and other holy days. Most activists, however, realized that if they shunned their heritage completely they would alienate their co-workers, and so they retained some traditional customs, such as speaking Yiddish.

Emma Goldman

Political activism earned many Jews a reputation as incendiary anarchists when, in fact, most were simply reformers. But some radicals did call for the overthrow of the U.S. government. The most famous of these agitators was Emma Goldman. Born in 1869, Goldman emigrated from her native country, Lithuania, at age 16. Employed for a few years in the garment industry in Rochester, New York, and New Haven, Connecticut, she then moved to New York City and was drawn into anarchism, a political movement that expounded opposition to all organized forms of government.

A gifted orator, Goldman attracted attention across the United States. In 1893, authorities imprisoned her for "inciting to riot" after she urged unemployed workers to steal bread if they were starving. From 1906 to 1917, she edited an anarchist monthly, *Mother Earth.* She became famous as a lecturer, "Red Emma," one of the greatest spellbinders in American history. Goldman embraced feminism, denouncing marriage as an institution that reduced women to the status of mere breeders. She encouraged women to use contraceptives in order to obtain their sexual freedom.

Her advocacy of birth control landed her behind bars again, in 1916. The next year she ran afoul of the law for obstructing the draft that inducted American soldiers into military service during World War I. In 1919, Goldman was stripped of her citizenship and deported to the Soviet Union, two years after its revolution installed the Communist regime. At first an enthusiastic supporter of the Soviet State, Goldman grew disenchanted with it, an experience she described in *My Disillusionment with Russia*, whose publication caused international furor. Thereafter she became a permanent exile, wandering from country to country until 1940, when she died in Toronto.

Union Days

Even Jewish-American organizers less radical than Goldman admired and romanticized the Russian Revolution. In fact, many turn-of-the-century Jewish immigrants had themselves fled Russia after the failure of its first revolution in 1905. These refugees arrived in America as sophisticated, experienced socialists with knowledge and skills that furthered the union movement. Greeted warmly by reformers in the United States, they worked alongside Jewish-American socialists and helped them transform a pool of disgruntled laborers into a formidable coalition.

One organization that profited from the expertise of Russian-Jewish activists was the International Ladies Garment Workers Union (ILGWU). Formed in 1900, it consisted of small unions that had struggled vainly for nearly a decade without winning concessions from clothing manufacturers. But aided by Russian immigrants, the ILGWU became a powerful force in organized labor, especially after a recession stung the American economy in 1907–08. News of the layoffs spread throughout the sweatshops, forcing panicked workers to confront the realization that the terms of their employment provided no guarantee of future welfare: If owners needed workers during a given week or month, they hired them; if not, the same laborers were fired without notice.

Uprisings

By 1909, after two years of unpredictable layoffs, garment workers had exhausted their tolerance. That spring and summer, Local 25, a branch of the ILGWU representing shirtwaist (blouse) makers, called a succession of isolated strikes, none of which persuaded manufacturing firms to recognize and deal with the union. Instead, owners hired professional thugs to frighten the laborers, most of whom were young immigrant women, some in their teens and twenties. This behavior seemed all the more appalling because the owners themselves often were Jews from eastern Europe.

Determined to save their strike, ILGWU leaders convened a union meeting in November 1909. They urged all the shirtwaist makers in New York City to walk off their jobs. The crowd—massed in a public-school assembly hall—resisted the plea, however, until a teenage firebrand named Clara Lemlich demanded immediate and forceful action. The thousands of women in the hall, whipped into a fury, vowed unanimously, "If I turn traitor to the cause I now pledge, may this hand wither from the arm I raise!"

The strikers returned to the streets, picketing tirelessly through the freezing winter despite the constant threat of beatings by hired goons and of imprisonment by antilabor courts. News of their plight penetrated New York's most prestigious neighborhoods, and rich women acted as patrons of the strikers, writing generous checks that aided the cause. In the end, though,

Two strikers walk the picket line in 1910.

the bravery and enthusiasm of the strikers brought only partial victory. When the walkout ended in February 1910, manufacturers agreed to provide improved work conditions but still refused to recognize the ILGWU. Nevertheless, the "Uprising of the Ten Thousand," as it was called, swelled the ranks of Local 25 from 100 to 10,000 members and, more important, gave strikers a power undreamed of just 3 months before. Newfound assurance and determination guided the union in its next mass protest, known as the "Great Revolt."

Unlike the relatively spontaneous Uprising, the Great Revolt culminated two years of careful planning by another segment of the garment industry, cloak makers. At its height, the protest involved some 30,000 workers. Later, Abraham Rosenberg, then president of the ILGWU, described the moment on July 1910 when the strikers poured out of their workplaces: "I could only picture to myself such a scene taking place when the Jews were led out of Egypt." Workers again demanded shorter hours, better wages, and a "closed shop"—a workplace that employed only union members. Against this third demand manufacturers argued that it would place companies totally at the mercy of the union and ultimately put them out of business. They had a point. In the garment industry competition between companies was fierce and bankruptcy a real possibility.

Themselves Russian Jews, manufacturers flinched at being labeled traitors to their own enslaved people. Indeed, outsiders often viewed the Great Revolt as a conflict pitting one set of Jews against another (despite a substantial minority of Italian workers in the "needle trades"), and New York's Jewish community hated the thought of providing a spectacle of grubby infighting for the amusement of the Gentile world. Many longed for a peaceful resolution to the conflict. As the summer of 1910 drew to a close, no settlement seemed imminent, and both sides agreed that a negotiator, Louis D. Brandeis, be brought in.

Louis D. Brandeis

Brandeis, a Bostonian, had already earned a reputation as "the People's Attorney." The son of leftist intellectuals from Germany, he was born in Louisville, Kentucky, in 1856. In 1875 he entered Harvard Law School, one of its few Jewish students, and finished his stay there with a record unsurpassed in the school's previous history. He set up a legal practice in Boston that soon thrived.

Despite his wealth, Brandeis clung to his family's tradition of liberal activism and frequently worked without pay for causes he deemed worthy. In 1907, for example, he challenged the attempt by industrial magnate J. P. Morgan to monopolize New England's railroads. Brandeis argued that big business, if unchecked, threatened the well-being both of individuals and of the

In March 1911, New York police guard the bodies of female workers killed during a fire at the Triangle Shirtwaist Company. This tragedy claimed the lives of 146 women and aroused great public sympathy for the union movement.

nation's economy. Later, Brandeis repeatedly took on large corporations in celebrated courtroom battles. As a result, he helped establish maximum working hours and minimum wages for all Americans.

In January 1916 Brandeis gained nationwide recognition when President Woodrow Wilson appointed him to the Supreme Court—the first Jew ever accorded this honor. But the nomination touched off bitter opposition from business leaders who regarded Brandeis as infuriatingly prolabor. Joined by anti-Semites within the government, the opponents of Brandeis shrilly claimed that his appointment to the bench would destroy the Republic. On June 1, 1916—after months of heated debate—the U.S. Senate finally approved Brandeis's nomination as Supreme Court justice, a post he held for 23 years.

At the time of the Great Revolt, Brandeis solidified his reputation as a fair and skillful negotiater. On September 2, 1910, he hammered out a compromise, called the Protocol of Peace, that allowed both camps—garment workers and manufacturers—to save face. The strikers received better wages and a work week shortened to 50 hours. (They had demanded 49.) And management accepted a "preferential union shop," a workplace where union members would be given first crack at jobs—in effect, a closed shop. Most important, the Protocol established methods of arbitration that paved the way for future disputes to be settled without the agony of strikes. The agreement secured a tremendous victory for Jewish labor. It would be years before all American corporations offered such decent terms to their workers.

The Socialist Age

A few weeks after the conclusion of the Great Revolt, its reverberations jolted the city of Chicago, where the third major Jewish strike of the period—involving 38,000 garment workers—broke out in the factories of a giant clothing manufacturer, Hart, Schaffner & Marx. This walkout led to an agreement reached largely through the cooperation of factory owner Joseph Schaffner. Berated by rabbis and social workers, Schaffner felt like a "moral failure" and admitted, "When I found out later of the conditions that had prevailed, I concluded that the strike should have occurred much sooner." The settlement, negotiated by Chicago workers, along with that of New York's Great Revolt, created precedents for arbitrating subsequent labor disputes.

The Uprising, Great Revolt, and Chicago strikes ushered in a grand era of Jewish socialism. In 1914, 1916, and again in 1920, New York's East Side elected socialist candidate Meyer London to Congress. In 1917, the New York branch of the party reached a height of electoral power: Socialist Morris Hillquit received 22 percent of the vote in New York's race for mayor, and the same election produced victories for 10 socialist assemblymen, 7 aldermen, and a municipal court judge.

But just when American socialists had begun to gain legitimacy, an internal conflict fissured the party. The problem traced back to Russia and its 1917 Revolution. One branch of that country's Socialist party, the Bolsheviks (led by the revolutionary Vladimir Ilyich Ulyanov—known as Lenin), had prevailed in a power struggle against the less radical Mensheviks. Both factions had supporters in the United States; each group argued that it represented "true" socialism, a claim that sometimes led to violent consequences.

In the 1920s, as infighting on the Left splintered the Socialist party, labor unions gradually moved toward the political center and into the mainstream of American politics. They received a boost in 1932 when Democratic presidential candidate Franklin Delano Roosevelt won the general election and instated policies heartily endorsed by labor leaders, some of whom he appointed to national office. Under the National Recovery Administration (NRA), established by Roosevelt to combat the hardships of the Great Depression, workers in the needle trades were gratified by wage increases ranging from 20 to 50 percent and by the introduction of the 35-hour workweek. (The latter measure is still in effect.)

Roosevelt's union backing mirrored his support among the Jewish-American community at large. Only a few decades earlier, the German-Jewish establishment had generally supported the Republicans, one of whom, President Theodore Roosevelt (Franklin's older cousin), had earned the Jews' admiration by appointing

An author as well as a politician, Morris Hillquit published History of Socialism in the United States *in 1903.*

Oscar S. Straus as secretary of commerce and labor, thereby giving the United States its first Jewish cabinet member.

But in the 1920s Jews shifted their loyalties to the Democratic party. In 1928, they rallied behind its presidential candidate Alfred E. Smith. (He was defeated by Republican Herbert Hoover.) Smith had spoken out vigorously against the anti-Semitic Ku Klux Klan (a group dating back to the Civil War, its first targets

On October 2, 1943, President Franklin D. Roosevelt appointed Judge Samuel I. Rosenman to the White House staff.

included Jews and Catholics as well as blacks), and his campaign manager was a prominent Jewish-American social reformer, Belle Moskowitz. Many Jews also approved of Smith's liberal policies, which called for social security, public health services, and prolabor legislation. In 1932 they were drawn for similar reasons to Franklin Roosevelt.

During Roosevelt's first bid for the presidency, his allies included various special interest groups—Catholics, laborers, and recent immigrants—but none backed him as enthusiastically as Jewish Americans. Even wealthy members of the community voted for him, whereas other groups tended to vote along class lines:

The rich cast their votes for Republicans, while the workers endorsed the Democrats.

As World War II approached and Roosevelt adopted the image of the great anti-Nazi warrior, his stature among Jews increased worldwide. Yet a terrible failure of Roosevelt's administration harmed the Jews incalculably during their greatest time of need. The U.S. government, ignoring desperate pleas from the Jewish-American community, refused to allow the persecuted Jews of Europe into the country, thus condemning thousands upon thousands to death. Even so, Jewish enthusiasm for Roosevelt never wavered. Each of the four times he ran for president he won an increasing number of Jewish votes, support that verged on adulation. Jewish Americans pointed with pride to Roosevelt's numerous and highly visible Jewish appointments to national office, including the cabinet and the Supreme Court. Indeed, some anti-Semites sneeringly referred to the New Deal as the Jew Deal.

Postwar Politics

In the years since Roosevelt's death, most Jews have continued to cast their vote for liberal and progressive presidential candidates. In 1952 they strongly favored Democrat Adlai Stevenson in his race against Dwight D. Eisenhower. And during the presidential elections of the 1960s, a majority of Jews supported Democrats John F. Kennedy, Lyndon B. Johnson, and Hubert H. Humphrey.

In the 1960s, Jewish voting reflected a widespread sympathy for the civil rights movement, which attempted to secure antidiscriminatory legislation and to guarantee voting rights for black Americans. In fact, as early as the 1930s, Jews had identified with racism directed against black Americans and worked to eliminate it. They helped found and direct the National Association for the Advancement of Colored People (NAACP), an organization led by Jewish presidents from 1930 to 1966. Civil rights leader Martin Luther

King, Jr., once remarked that "it would be impossible to record the contribution that the Jewish people have made toward the Negro's struggle for freedom—it has been so great." In the late 1960s, Jews stood at the forefront of protests against the Vietnam War. One of the most powerful antiwar organizations, Students for a Democratic Society (SDS), counted among its leaders three young Jewish radicals—Abbie Hoffman, Jerry Rubin, and Mark Rudd.

The causes of Jewish progressivism have long been a matter of debate. Some analysts think that Jews perceive in liberal social programs a reflection of the ethical and charitable beliefs woven into ancient Jewish teaching. Irving Howe, author of *World of Our Fathers*, a study of Jewish immigrants in the United States, has suggested that the liberalism of postwar American Jews "was based on at least two factors: the once-powerful tradition of secular Jewish socialism, now fading but still felt and remembered . . . and the premise, shared by Jews in the West for perhaps two centuries, that

Many prominent Jewish Americans joined with Martin Luther King, Jr., on his historic 1965 march between the Alabama cities of Selma and Montgomery.

*Abbie Hoffman, a leader of the
student movement that opposed
the Vietnam War, points to a
photo of himself as a teenager.*

Jewish interests and indeed, survival were best served
by an open, secular society promoting liberal values and
tolerating a diversity of religious groups."

Other writers have seen the Jews' liberal commitment primarily as a response to anti-Semitism, an evil
that still haunts America. As long as Jews fear an up-
surge of intolerance toward them, as long as pockets of
discrimination (such as all-Gentile country clubs) still
exist, Jews will probably continue giving their support
to the politicians they regard as the staunchest defend-
ers of civil liberties. ∾

JEWISH CULTURE, AMERICAN CULTURE

Jews have played an enormous role in shaping 20th-century American culture. Our theater, fiction, painting, rock and roll, and, above all, our films bear an unmistakably Jewish-American stamp. But the first flowering of Jewish culture in this country—the literature of eastern European immigrants—remained inaccessible to the mainstream of American society for years because it was written in Yiddish, not English.

The earliest Jewish-American writers often reached their public through the Yiddish newspapers, which included the work of fine poets, some of them members of the "Sweatshop School," which detailed the hardships of life in New York City's garment factories. One of the most memorable lyrics in this tradition, "Meine Yingele" ("My Little Boy"), describes a father's sadness at leaving for work at dawn and returning home after dark, thus never seeing his child awake. Later Yiddish poets grafted modern techniques on to their verse, yet they still failed to find an audience among the more sophisticated first-generation Jewish Americans, whose first language usually was English. As the use of Yiddish declined in America, the work of these poets faded from view.

Isaac Bashevis Singer has written folktales for children as well as novels for adults.

Not all Yiddish writers vanished without a trace, however. Some produced fiction that earned a wider following on both sides of the Atlantic; later, their translated works became popular with an even more diverse audience. By the late 1800s, European Yiddish literature could claim some major novelists, some of whom made America their home.

Yiddish Fiction

When he arrived at Ellis Island from Russia at the turn of the 20th century, Sholom Aleichem already commanded a reputation as the outstanding Yiddish writer of his day. In fact, his novels, plays, and short stories helped alert readers to the intrinsic literary merits of the Yiddish tongue. In America, some of Aleichem's 300 short stories immediately found a home in the Yiddish newspapers published in New York City. Aleichem's wry tales, set in the shtetls of Russia, describe the lives of downtrodden Jews, including Tevye the Dairyman, who decades later captivated Broadway as the title character of the musical *Fiddler on the Roof.*

Even greater popularity greeted two later Yiddish novelists, the Singer brothers—Israel Joshua and Isaac Bashevis. They were born in Poland—Israel in 1893, Isaac in 1904—the sons of a rabbi, and at an early age they were introduced to Jewish scholarship and folklore. I. J. Singer's Yiddish stories preceded him to America, where they attracted the attention of *Jewish Daily Forward* editor Abraham Cahan, who hired Singer—then based in eastern Europe—to serve as the paper's Polish correspondent. Singer eventually emigrated to New York in 1934 and there completed his masterpiece, *The Brothers Ashkenazi,* a massive family chronicle that in translation gained popularity with American readers.

His younger brother, Isaac Bashevis Singer, observed Jewish life in urban Warsaw and in the homely shtetl where his grandfather lived. Urged by his parents to become a rabbi, I. B. Singer instead modeled himself after his older brother and dedicated himself to writing fiction. At first he wrote in Hebrew, but soon decided it was a dead language (later it was revived as the national language of Israel), switching to his native tongue, Yiddish. Singer immigrated to the United States the year after his brother and, like him, began contributing to the *Jewish Daily Forward*, where many of his stories and novels made their debut.

Isaac Bashevis Singer's fiction combines realism and folklore and explores the Jews' sadness at the decline of their traditional culture—a loss that Singer himself felt acutely as a writer of a dying language, for Yiddish ultimately proved even more perishable than Hebrew. Singer's own writing owed much to English translators, who introduced to a large American audience classic stories such as "Gimpel the Fool" (brilliantly translated by another giant of Jewish-American literature, Saul Bellow) and novels such as *Satan in Goray* and *The Family Moskat*. In 1978, I. B. Singer became the first Yiddish writer to be awarded the Nobel Prize for literature.

The Early Jewish Theater

Jewish culture includes no formal theatrical tradition apart from the comic playlets that annually commemorate Purim, the holiday celebrating the deliverance of ancient Jews from a massacre by the Persians. Yet dramatic theater, more than any other art form, captured the collective imagination of America's early Jewish immigrants. Written and performed in Yiddish, these productions made no pretensions to sophistication but gave their rapt audiences colorful and emotional displays that distilled the daily passions of immigrant life. Some devout Jews found theater immoral, and cultivated German Jews shuddered at the coarseness of the productions, but most immigrants from eastern Europe loved them.

In the late 19th century, Yiddish performing troupes started to appear on both sides of the Atlantic, staging New York's first Yiddish production in 1882. Theaters cropped up wherever an audience of Jews could be assembled. The earliest plays—a hodge-podge of historical themes, farce, music, melodrama, and local jokes—poured out of the pens of hacks who feverishly recycled antique plots. A playwright who needed a high-flown speech might steal some eloquent fire from Shakespeare or Goethe. Other dramatists simply wrenched masterpieces of world drama into Jewish settings or, in a spasm of ambition, presented them more "seriously" as translations. (An audience at the opening of a Yiddish *Hamlet* was so impressed that it called for the author to take a bow.) These renditions inevitably relied on spectacle and emotion to stir the audience, but the success of nearly any production was guaranteed if it focused on two themes, Jewish suffering and Jewish endurance.

Yiddish theater lacked brilliant playwrights, but it teemed with marvelous actors, men and women magically adept at plumbing humor and tragedy from even the most threadbare scripts. Wizards at improvisation, Yiddish actors nightly invented gems of dialogue far superior to the playwrights' wooden words, a skill that sometimes drove Yiddish playwrights into fits of rage. One dramatist, onstage in his own play, became infuriated when an actress improvised an aside to the audience. "Stop it," he yelled, banging his fist on a table, "that's not in the script!"

Playwrights might fume, but playgoers relished these freewheeling performances. Jewish-American audiences of this era were, by and large, an unbuttoned and raucous lot. They munched on snacks, chatted with neighbors, and drowned out villains with their hisses. Yet their appetite for theater far surpassed that of more elite audiences, and they could be deeply moved, often to tears, by what they saw. At a performance of *The Jewish King Lear*, one man was so distraught by the spectacle of filial ingratitude that he rushed up to the stage shouting, "To hell with your stingy daughter! She has a stone, not a heart!"

Gradually, the Yiddish theater—both in America and in eastern Europe—acquired sophistication, influenced by the masterful 19th-century dramas of the Norwegian Henrik Ibsen, the Swede August Strindberg, and the Russian Anton Chekhov. Still, it never won a place among the great theatrical traditions of the West. Like Yiddish poetry and fiction, Jewish drama reached its maturity in the same moment that its parent culture faded. In America, Jews adopted English as their native tongue, often shunning the Old World language; in Eu-

New York's Grand Theatre featured Yiddish stage-idol Jacob Adler in a 1903 production of In the Broken Hearts.

Jewish-American comedienne Fanny Brice (right) starred with actress Judy Garland in the 1937 motion picture Everybody Sing.

rope, the Nazi holocaust wiped out most of the Jewish population. After the 1940s no Yiddish-speaking audience existed, and this vibrant theatrical tradition died.

The Age of Vaudeville

Jewish-American performers succeeded, however, in carrying their art beyond the immigrant community. Indeed, the full flowering of the Yiddish theater coincided with the great age of vaudeville, an American-grown variety of music-hall entertainment. Many Jewish-American performers, comfortable with English, crossed over into this popular area of show business. Fanny Brice, the funniest Jewish comedienne of her age, burlesqued Jewish immigrant culture with Yiddish-accent routines that delighted fans of all ethnic backgrounds. Thousands of them flocked to see her act at the Ziegfeld Follies—the spectacular revue put together by the impresario Florenz Ziegfeld, himself a Jew. (Decades later, Barbra Streisand, another Jewish star, portrayed Brice first on Broadway and then on screen in the musical *Funny Girl*.)

The vaudeville era (approximately 1880–1930) claimed a host of great Jewish comics and song-and-dance men, including Eddie Cantor, George Burns, and Jack Benny. The Marx Brothers (Groucho, Harpo, Chico, and Zeppo), originated their comic style on the vaudeville stage, then starred in filmed versions of their musical hits, *The Cocoanuts* and *Animal Crackers*, which

A publicity photo taken during the 1930s on the Metro-Goldwyn-Mayer lot features three of the four Marx Brothers (from left): Harpo, Groucho, and Chico.

launched their Hollywood careers. Such Marx Brothers classics as *Duck Soup* (1933) and *A Night at the Opera* (1935) remain unsurpassed as hilarious lampoons of American society, especially its upper echelons.

Jewish-American comedy flourished also in the stand-up routines of Henny Youngman and Myron Cohen and in the daring monologues of Lenny Bruce. Other Jewish-American performers—such as Sid Caesar, Joan Rivers, and Buddy Hackett—had great success on television. Many of these later comedians cut their teeth performing in the "Borscht Belt," the string of Jewish resorts in New York State's Catskill mountains. Mel Brooks and Woody Allen, who both got their start in the "mountains," went on to stellar careers in the movies. And one of the Borscht Belt's enduring comedians, Jackie Mason, has brought his unique routine to the Broadway stage, delighting Jews and Gentiles alike.

Jewish-American Songwriters

Just as Jewish Americans have helped shape our sense of humor, they have contributed enormously to Broadway musicals and to the nation's storehouse of popular tunes. In the early 20th century no performer pleased audiences more than singer Al Jolson. A veteran of circuses, minstrel shows, and vaudeville, he debuted on Broadway in 1911 in *La Belle Paree*. In 1927, Jolson made cinema history with his portrayal of a cantor's son in the autobiographical film *The Jazz Singer*, the first feature-length "talkie." Jolson's rendition of the sentimental song "Mammie" entranced filmgoers accustomed to the silent screen and forced Hollywood's major studios to switch to the production of sound movies.

In the early 1900s, before technology could adequately reproduce sound, families created their own musical entertainment at home on the parlor piano, often using sheet music that spelled out the words and

notes of America's latest hits. Many of these tunes originated in the offices of music publishers clustered together on New York City's 28th Street, known jokingly as "Tin Pan Alley" because many of the songs cranked out there had all the grace of clattering cookware.

In the first quarter of the 20th century, Tin Pan Alley was home to many Jewish Americans. Songwriters of German or eastern European descent composed favorites such as "Waltz Me Around Again, Willie" and "Those Wedding Bells Shall Not Ring Out," songs that earned large sums for their publishers. The Alley also served as a training ground for talented young musicians, including a high-school dropout who eventually became one of America's leading composers.

Born in 1898 to Russian immigrant parents, George Gershwin (born Jakob Bruskin Gershvin) was barely 20 when he wrote his first hit, "Swanee," sung by Al Jolson. Within a few years, his star had ascended to Broadway, where his jazz-flavored scores energized musical

In 1936, Al Jolson (in "blackface," holding hat) starred with big-band leader Cab Calloway in the Warner Brothers musical The Singing Kid.

theater. In collaboration with his brother, Ira, a lyricist, Gershwin composed songs ("I Got Rhythm," "Love Is Here to Stay," "They Can't Take That Away from Me") that graced the repertoires of Billie Holiday, Ella Fitzgerald, Frank Sinatra, and other popular singers.

But Gershwin's true genius came to light in the classical concert hall. His symphonic compositions—especially *Rhapsody in Blue* and *An American in Paris*—lent new respectability to jazz, a purely American art form. His 1935 opera *Porgy and Bess*, which included the lilting air "Summertime," depicted the lives of poor blacks in Charleston, South Carolina. He completed this, his most ambitious work, at age 37—just two years before he died in Hollywood, California, of a brain tumor.

Gershwin's contemporary, Richard Rodgers, also brought innovations to the musical theater. Teamed with lyricist Lorenz Hart and, later, with Oscar Hammerstein II, Rodgers produced some of the most successful shows in Broadway history, among them *Oklahoma!* (1943), which incorporated themes of American folk music—a daring experiment for its time. Another of the greatest songwriters of the early century was Irving Berlin, who gave us "God Bless America" and "White Christmas."

In May 1982, pianist Vladimir Horowitz practiced in preparation for his first English recital in 30 years.

Classical-Music Artists

The oustanding heir to Gershwin's concert-hall legacy
is Leonard Bernstein—conductor, composer, and pianist. Bernstein was born in Lawrence, Massachusetts,
in 1918, the son of Russian Jews. After completing
undergraduate work at Harvard, he defied the wishes
of his father by pursuing a career in music. Bernstein
attended the prestigious Curtis Institute of Music, in
Philadelphia, then studied conducting under the mae-
stro Serge Koussevitsky, and later became his assistant
at the Boston Symphony, a position coveted by many
young conductors. Just one year later, that post led
Bernstein to an appointment as assistant conductor of
the New York Philharmonic. Shortly afterward, he won
almost overnight acclaim when the orchestra's conductor, Bruno Walter, could not appear at a performance
and Bernstein stepped in for him, masterfully leading
the Philharmonic through its program.

At the age of 40, Bernstein was appointed music
director of the New York Philharmonic—the first
American-born musician to hold that position with a
major U.S. orchestra. Soon he began to compose or-
chestral music as well as conduct it. His ballet *Fancy
Free* met with such success that he expanded it—col-
laborating with choreographer Jerome Robbins—into
the hit musical *On the Town*. Still, Bernstein's Broadway career took a backseat to his other musical pursuits
until 1957, the year the curtain rose on his *West Side
Story*, a musical updating of Shakespeare's *Romeo and
Juliet*. In 1961, Hollywood brought *West Side Story* to
a wider audience with a film version that earned four
Academy Awards.

The contributions of Jews to classical music is most
evident among performers. A brief list of virtuosos includes the pianists Vladimir Horowitz, Rudolf Serkin,
and Gary Graffman; the violinists Jascha Heifetz, Ye-
hudi Menuhin, Itzhak Perlman, and Isaac Stern; the
cellist Leonard Rose; and the singers Robert Merrill,
Roberta Peters, and Beverly Sills.

One of the most remarkable Jewish performers of recent times was the Canadian pianist and composer Glenn Gould. Born in 1932 in Toronto, Ontario, Gould was a child prodigy. By age 12 he was studying at the Royal Conservatory of Music in Toronto; at age 14 he debuted as a piano soloist with the Toronto Symphony; and when only 19 years old he began touring nationally. He earned a worldwide reputation as an innovative interpreter of the 18th-century composer Johann Sebastian Bach. At the same time Gould created his own works, the first of which—written for a string quartet—premiered in 1956. Today Gould is remembered as a studio artist who surprised his followers by quitting the concert hall in the mid-1960s. Thereafter he became immersed in the intricacies of recording and logged countless hours in the studio, braiding together strands of taped performances until he produced a rendition of unparalleled precision and sensitivity. Gould was only 50 when he died in 1982, just months after he had rounded out his career by recording Bach's *Goldberg Variations*, a complex piece he had first put on disk 25 years before.

Jewish Folk and Rock Stars

The most recognizable Jewish names in the field of music belong not to classical performers but to a pantheon of folk and rock stars. These luminaries include Paul Simon and Art Garfunkel, Carole King, Cass Elliot (of the Mamas and the Papas), Phil Ochs, and Robert Zimmerman—better known as Bob Dylan, perhaps the most important writer and performer in the history of American popular music.

In 1960, Dylan—a native of the mining town of Hibbing, Minnesota—arrived in New York City's Greenwich Village at the age of 19, toting an acoustic guitar and a repertory of tall tales about his past: He claimed to have run away from home and joined the circus at an early age and also to have known and played with Big Joe Williams and other blues titans. Soon Dylan landed spots in small clubs, and from the outset he stood apart from the purists who had dominated the insular folk scene since the early 1950s. Clad in blue jeans, boots, a suede jacket, and his signature corduroy cap, Dylan croaked out powerful songs in a rough hewn voice that mingled passion and cunning.

The most riveting performer of folk music, Dylan quickly became its most inspired composer, a troubadour whose image-drenched lyrics assaulted the wrongs of American society—racial prejudice, economic injustice, militarism, and more. "Blowin' in the Wind," his first hit—and perhaps still his best known—emerged as the anthem of the civil rights movement in the 1960s. "The Times They Are A-Changin'" heralded the era of student protest.

In the mid-1960s, Dylan moved beyond overtly political tunes and began creating a body of work that earned him a reputation as a poet as well as songwriter. He backed his new lyrics with a rock-and-roll band, much to the dismay of fans who felt he had abandoned his true calling as a folk artist in order to reap the rewards of commercial stardom. For the first time, Dylan began to hear heckling and catcalls at his concerts. Undaunted, he refused to cater to his old devotees, and in subsequent years his career was highlighted by mercurial changes in style and subject matter. After a motorcycle accident in 1966, Dylan began studying the Bible, which he later called "the most underrated and overrated book in history," and made several trips to Israel. At the end of the 1970s Dylan again surprised his fans by becoming a "born-again" Christian. His devotional lyrics of this phase yielded at least two masterpieces, "I Believe in You" and "Every Grain of Sand."

Although not as prolific as he once was, Dylan today ranks among the major artists of his time. His lyrics have been lavishly praised by such eminent authors as Norman Mailer and Joyce Carol Oates and analyzed by literary critics such as the Cambridge University professor Christopher Ricks. More than any other rock musician, Dylan has proved that a rock-and-roll song can be a poetic creation.

In 1962, Bob Dylan released his first album, Bob Dylan, *a collection that included many traditional folk songs.*

Hollywood

Jewish Americans have enriched nearly every realm of American culture, but none more so than film. In fact, Jews formed, then ruled, all but one of Hollywood's production companies in the "golden age" of the movies, the 1920s and 1930s. The Goldwyn and Mayer of Metro-Goldwyn-Mayer, the Fox of 20th Century-Fox, the Warner Brothers (Sam, Jack, Albert, and Harry), and Paramount's chief, Adolph Zukor, all claimed Jewish heritage. Most of these movie moguls were born to poverty in eastern Europe, immigrating to America at an early age. Restless young men, they drifted into various jobs before discovering that a fortune lay in "nickelodeons," America's first movie theaters. These primitive cinemas typically consisted of a rented storefront and rows of wooden chairs on which audiences sat for hours, entranced by silent movies. As nickelodeons drew larger and steadier audiences, owners built more theaters, often sprucing them up into showy palaces that attracted a more discriminating crowd. Soon their profits soared, and entrepreneurs moved first into film distribution, then into production. By the 1920s, motion pictures had grown into a million-dollar industry presided over by immigrants.

It is remarkable that these upstarts—with their miserable educations, Yiddish accents, and unabashed love of money—molded America's popular taste more forcefully than anyone else in the 20th century. For the Hollywood moguls ruled with an iron fist, imprinting their vision on every film released by their studios. And it is a tribute to these men that they innately understood the fantasies that touched the imaginations of a huge and diverse nation.

Two memorable moguls were Irving Grant Thalberg, the "boy wonder," and David Oliver Selznick (1902–65), young mavericks who dominated Hollywood during its heyday in the 1930s. Born in Brooklyn, New York, in 1899, Thalberg struck out for Hollywood while still a teenager and found work in Universal Stu-

dios. At 25 he became production manager of Metro-Goldwyn-Mayer and directed the studio toward making high-toned films, usually based on literary classics or current best-sellers. His successes included *Grand Hotel* (1932), *Mutiny on the Bounty* (1935), and *Romeo and Juliet*—which premiered in 1936, the year of his untimely death. Thalberg inspired novelist F. Scott Fitzgerald to create a similar character, Monroe Stahr, in *The Last Tycoon*, an unfinished novel set in Hollywood. Describing Stahr, Fitzgerald wrote: "He cherished the parvenu's passionate loyalty to an imaginary past."

Thalberg's contemporary and sometime colleague at Metro-Goldwyn-Mayer, David O. Selznick, hailed from Pittsburgh and was the son of Lewis J. Selznick, a motion-picture producer forced out of Hollywood when competition there became fierce during the 1920s. Unlike Thalberg, who threw in his lot with a single company, the younger Selznick jumped from studio to studio. Between 1926 and 1933 he worked on the staff of Metro-Goldwyn-Mayer, Paramount Pictures, and RKO Radio Pictures, returning to M-G-M in 1933. Two years later he founded Selznick International Pictures. Most movie fans know Selznick as the producer of the film epic *Gone with the Wind* (1933), but his credits also include *Anna Karenina* (1935), *Tom Sawyer* (1937), and *A Farewell to Arms* (1943), all based on literary classics.

Thalberg, Selznick, and other moguls seldom hid their own Jewish roots, yet they painstakingly suppressed all traces of Jewishness in their movies. The same secrecy was practiced by many successful Jewish-American directors, screenwriters, and actors. Even today audiences seldom are aware that they are seeing the work of Jews when they enjoy a performance by Lauren Bacall (Betty Joan Perske), James Caan, Tony Curtis (Bernie Schwartz), Kirk Douglas (Issur Danielovich Demsky), Richard Dreyfuss, Peter Falk, Elliot Gould (Elliot Goldstein), Goldie Hawn, Dustin Hoffman, Madeline Kahn, Danny Kaye (Danny Kominski), Jerry Lewis, the Marx Brothers, Walter Matthau, Bette Midler, Paul Muni (Muni Weisenfreund), Paul Newman, Edward G. Robinson, Rod Steiger, Gene Wilder (Gene Silverstein), or Shelley Winters (Shirley Schrift), among other top box-office draws.

Many of these stars worked under the guidance of famous Jewish directors: Josef von Sternberg, Erich von Stroheim, Ernst Lubitsch, George Cukor, Sidney Lumet, Paul Mazursky, Mike Nichols, and Steven Spielberg. Their European colleagues Fritz Lang, Otto Preminger, and Billy Wilder (first a screenwriter, then a director) came to the United States during World War II to escape from Hitler, as did some of Hollywood's greatest composers and cameramen. Hollywood also boasts some famous converts to Judaism: Marilyn Monroe, Elizabeth Taylor, and Sammy Davis, Jr.

Woody Allen

Hollywood's greatest Jewish-American star has made no effort whatsoever to disguise his origins. Woody Allen was born Allen Stewart Konigsberg in Brooklyn, New York, in 1935. After dropping out of college, he wrote comic routines for several popular comedians,

Woody Allen plays his clarinet at Michael's Pub, a New York cabaret where he regularly performs on Monday nights.

including Sid Caesar, the star of television's hit variety program "Your Show of Shows." In 1961, Allen polished his own stand-up routine, delighting audiences across the country, though he sometimes was so paralyzed by stage fright that he literally had to be pushed onstage.

In his stand-up monologues, Allen developed the character of the incompetent loser—or *nebbish* in Yiddish. Later this character became the centerpiece of his movies. After writing and appearing in a couple of films, he made his debut as a director in 1969 with *Take the Money and Run*, the first of many cinematic successes. Within a decade Allen was regarded not only as America's leading film comedian but as one of its finest directors. In 1978 he won Academy Awards for best director, best screenplay, and best picture for *Annie Hall*. In 1987 he again earned an Oscar, this time for his screenplay for *Hannah and Her Sisters*. Allen's humor often pokes fun at the anxieties, obsessions, and preoccupations of intellectual urbanites—themes rooted in his experience as a New York Jew but nevertheless accessible to a wide audience both in the United States and abroad.

Jewish Fiction

Woody Allen is not alone in delineating the Jewish-American psyche. Indeed, his movies owe much to the distinguished body of Jewish-American literature. The first Jewish-American works usually were straightforward portrayals of the immigrant experience, such as Abraham Cahan's *The Rise of David Levinsky*, published in 1917. Later novels, such as Daniel Fuchs's *Williamsburg Trilogy* (1934–37) and Henry Roth's *Call It Sleep* (1939), probed more subtly into the Jewish-American psyche. Their contemporary Nathanael West shied away from overtly Jewish themes, but in his masterpiece *Miss Lonelyhearts* (1933) he perfectly captured the anxiety of depression America, a place ruled by false hopes and unrealized dreams.

The next generation of Jewish-American novelists went further in their explorations. They sought to relate their people's experience not only by incorporating plots, characters, and themes that typified Jewish life but by forging a new idiom—or style—that echoed the rhythms of immigrant English and restored to American prose the vitality of the spoken word. Canadian-born novelist Saul Bellow deserves the greatest credit for this innovation.

The son of Russian Jews, Bellow moved to Chicago in 1923 at age eight and in 1987 lived there still. His mixture of linguistic influences—Yiddish and Chicagoese—provides a counterpoint to his great erudition and intelligence and has given rise to what one critic has called "the first major new style in American prose fiction since those of Hemingway and Faulkner: a mingling of high-flown intellectual bravado with racy-tough street Jewishness." In Bellow's 1953 novel *The Adventures of Augie March*, the narrator describes the city of Chicago with both humor and anguish:

> Around was Chicago. In its repetition it exhausted your imagination of details and units, more units than the cells of the brain and bricks of Babel . . . A mysterious tremor, dust, vapor, emanation of stupendous effort traveled with the air, over me . . . and over the clinics, clinks, factories, flophouses, morgue, skid row. As before the work of Egypt and Assyria, as before a sea, you're nothing here. Nothing.

Bellow's other novels, including *Seize the Day*, *Herzog*, and *Humboldt's Gift*, brim with manic energy and self-lacerating introspection. One of the leading novelists of his generation, he won the Nobel Prize for literature in 1976.

Bellow's companions in the Jewish-American literary canon make good company indeed. Brooklyn-born Bernard Malamud wrote gripping narratives that hark back to the time-weathered tradition of Yiddish folk stories and dignify the ordinary man. His novels include *The Assistant*, *The Fixer*, and *The Tenants*. In *Portnoy's*

Complaint, Philip Roth burlesques middle-class Jewish culture with outrageous humor. Norman Mailer is as famous for his pugnacious personality as for his first-class novels (*The Naked and the Dead*) and journalism (*The Executioner's Song*). J. D. Salinger produced an American classic in *Catcher in the Rye* and chronicled the lives of the part-Jewish Glass family in his novel *Franny and Zooey*; and Cynthia Ozick, the most devout of major Jewish-American writers, has written several short-story collections, such as *The Pagan Rabbi*, whose characters await moments of elevating self-discovery and religious revelation.

Jews have also contributed to American poetry. Allen Ginsberg commands perhaps the widest following of contemporary Jewish verse writers. His most celebrated work, *Howl*, attacks American materialism and seemed to speak for a disillusioned generation when it appeared in 1956. Five years later, Ginsberg wrote *Kaddish* (Hebrew for the ancient prayer for the dead) as an elegy to his mother—a Russian immigrant who suffered from mental illness her entire life.

In the 1960s, Ginsberg publicly proclaimed his homosexuality, long before gay liberation was a household term, and also became a fixture of the counterculture, inventing the term *flower power*. In the tradition of Jewish leftists and of his own family (he described his background as "Jewish left-wing atheist Russian"), he crusaded against the Vietnam War. He once defended his unconventional style by telling critics, "If I look funny or get up in public and say I am homosexual, take drugs, and hear Blake's voice, then people who are heterosexual, don't take drugs, and hear Shakespeare's voice may feel freer to do what they want and be what they are."

The Fine Arts

Jewish-American writers trace their roots to a long Hebrew and Yiddish literary tradition, but no such tradition exists in the visual arts. The Old Testament commandment "Thou shalt not make unto thee any

Cynthia Ozick's novel The Messiah of Stockholm *met with great critical acclaim when it was published in 1987.*

Followers surround poet Alan Ginsberg as he chants a mantra in London's Hyde Park in 1967.

graven images, or any likeness of anything" (Exodus 20:4) reverberated through centuries of Jewish culture. With few exceptions—such as decorations on the Torah or the illustrations in the Haggadah, a special prayer book used at the Passover feast—Jews traditionally were not exposed to drawing or painting.

In America that circumstance changed. In 1889, the Educational Alliance on the Lower East Side of New York, financed with the money of assimilated German Jews, opened its doors and offered courses in various disciplines, including fine arts, to eastern European immigrants. These classes evolved into the Alliance Art School, a training ground for some of the country's finest Jewish artists: Ben Shahn, Adolph Gottlieb, Louise Nevelson, Barnett Newman, and Mark Rothko, among others.

In New York especially, Jewish Americans helped usher in modern art, introducing it to the public through exhibits at places such as Gallery 291, operated by a German-Jewish photographer named Alfred Stieglitz. Among the new artists Stieglitz exhibited were two from the immigrant East Side, Max Weber and Abraham Walkowitz. Both had made the journey from New York to Paris to study art—a long way, culturally, for poor Jewish Americans to travel—and both influenced

the development of 20th-century American painters, one of whom was fellow New Yorker Ben Shahn.

Shahn was born in Lithuania in 1898 and immigrated to New York City with his parents in 1906. As a young man, he got a firsthand glimpse of Jewish socialism and as an adult ardently supported left-wing causes. In fact, Shahn first gained artistic recognition with a series of works inspired by a liberal cause célèbre, the Massachusetts state government's 1927 execution of two Italian anarchists named Nicola Sacco and Bartolomeo Vanzetti. His painting *The Passion of Sacco and Vanzetti* now hangs in New York's Whitney Museum.

Shahn's early training as a lithographer instilled in him a strong sense of graphic design, a talent reflected in his many posters. During the 1930s the Farm Security Administration hired him as a photographer, an assignment requiring him to record the rural poverty of America. As a muralist, he assisted Mexican artist Diego Rivera on his commissioned works for the RCA Building in Rockefeller Center. Despite his worldly ex-

Painter Mark Rothko was a leading figure in the "New York School" that dominated the art world in the 1950s.

perience, Shahn never forgot his Jewish origins, and later in his career he designed stained-glass windows for the Temple Beth Israel in Buffalo, New York, and illustrated a Passover Haggadah.

Not all artistic activity occurred in New York. Early in the 20th century Paris became a mecca for avant-garde Americans and the group's catalyst, Gertrude Stein. Born in Allegheny, Pennsylvania, in 1874, to German-Jewish parents, Stein grew up mainly in Oakland, California. At Radcliffe College she studied psychology with William James, one of the discipline's leading theorists. In 1903 she moved to Paris and lived there until her death in 1946. Her copious writings include such masterpieces as *Three Lives* (1909) and *The Autobiography of Alice B. Toklas* (1933). Stein earned equal renown for presiding over a salon that in the 1920s became a second home to many talented Americans living in Paris. She helped Ernest Hemingway, Sherwood Anderson, and other writers find a larger public and supported such great European painters as Pablo Picasso, Henri Matisse, and Paul Cézanne.

Because no formal tradition restrained them, Jewish Americans were more inclined than others to embrace avant-garde styles when the currents of modernism swept the art world in the early 1900s. Jewish artists participated in the revolutionary movement that followed World War II, abstract expressionism, which broke free of the limitations imposed by conventional realism and its attempt to act as a mirror of the objective world. Leading abstract artists included Adolph Gottlieb, Mark Rothko, and Barnett Newman, as well as Lee Krasner and Franz Kline.

From the overheated melodrama of Yiddish theater to the mass-produced fantasies of Hollywood to the complex distortions of modern painting, the Jewish-American influence on our country's art has ranged far and wide, encompassing a vast array of experience. This ethnic group has contributed much to the intellectual and cultural life of North America and seems likely to guide it for years to come. ⚬

A group of rabbinical students study the Torah.

AT HOME IN THE NEW WORLD

No ethnic group has ever had more reason to leave the Old World than the Jews. Denied a homeland for thousands of years, forced onto the margins of hostile societies, these persecuted people seemed ideally suited to make a fresh start in North America. Yet Jewish immigration to the New World began fairly recently. A mere handful arrived before the mid-19th century, and the numbers remained small until the 1880s, when Jews first arrived in force.

The reason for this delayed immigration is that, unlike other refugees from overcrowded or repressive lands, Jews had grown so used to persecution that they accepted it as their assigned fate. The history of Judaism records, in large part, the history of anti-Semitism. From the Spanish Inquisition to the Nazis' "final solution," Jews have suffered irrational and brutal attacks meant to destroy their entire culture. Only when conditions became unbearable in eastern Europe—where the majority of the population lived in the late 19th century—did Jews make a concerted effort to tear off the shackles of Old World bigotry.

Once the exodus began, however, it was prodigious. Between 1880 and 1920 more than 3.5 million Jews arrived on our shores. Within a generation they had transformed their new homeland beyond reckoning, and they continue to do so. In areas as diverse as banking and filmmaking, Jewish Americans have made contributions that far outweigh their numbers. Today, 100 years after the first great wave of newcomers climbed out of steerage, Jewish Americans stand as an example for later immigrant groups who hope to attain equal success.

Spectacular as that success has been, it came only after a struggle. American anti-Semitism, though seldom as virulent as its European version, nonetheless existed for the first immigrants, just as it does for their descendants. Until recently, quotas locked worthy Jews out of the choicest schools and professions, and the first generations of immigrants resigned themselves to lives spent in demoralizing tenements in America's great cities. Even after Jewish Americans rose out of the ghetto and into the comfortable middle class, they could only manage an impotent protest when the U.S. goverment turned away a boatload of refugees from Germany, thus sentencing them to extermination in Nazi death camps. A year does not go by without anti-Semitism rearing its ugly head—a swastika spray painted on the wall of a suburban temple, a slur uttered publicly by a prominent public figure.

For the most part, however, America has been uncommonly generous to people of Jewish ancestry, more generous than any other nation in history. Indeed, the greatest threat posed to Jews who have remade their lives in America is not exclusion from the mainstream but its opposite, assimilation. In many ways America has been so good to Jews, so welcoming, that the community runs the risk of losing touch with the tragic reality of its unique history. As Irving Howe has written in *World of Our Fathers*:

> America exacted a price. Not that it "demanded" that
> the immigrant Jews repudiate their past, their religion,
> or their culture; nor that it "insisted" they give up
> the marks of their spiritual distinctiveness. American
> society, by its very nature, simply made it all but
> impossible for the culture of Yiddish to survive. It set
> for the east European Jews a trap or lure of the most

A mother and daughter pause during a stroll across the Williamsburg Bridge, which connects New York City's Lower East Side and Brooklyn.

pleasant kind. It allowed the Jews a life far more "normal" than anything their most visionary programs had foreseen, and all that it asked—it did not even ask, it merely rendered easy and persuasive—was that the Jews surrender their collective self.

Not all Jewish Americans would agree with this assessment. *Surrender* is a strong word. But few members of this ethnic group would deny that acceptance and success have come at a cost. Any reader of fiction by Saul Bellow, Cynthia Ozick, or Philip Roth, any moviegoer who laughs delightedly at the self-mocking witticisms of Woody Allen, knows that a germ of uneasiness eats away at these brilliant artists, as it eats away at most Jewish Americans. Few of the "chosen people" can escape the searing memory of the Holocaust or the awareness that the security of life in North America is soberly balanced by the tenuous future of Israel.

Judaism is a faith founded on historical consciousness, and as long as Jewish Americans remember their past and their connection to embattled Jewish communities that exist in isolated pockets of the world, this remarkable people will continue to thrive. And someday, perhaps, other nations will study the example of America, which has been so amply served by the Jews whom it welcomed and encouraged. ≈

FURTHER READING

Bellow, Saul. *The Adventures of Augie March.* New York: Viking Press, 1954.

Birmingham, Stephen. *Our Crowd: The Great Jewish Families of New York.* New York: Harper & Row, 1967.

———. *The Rest of Us: The Rise of America's Eastern European Jews.* Boston: Little, Brown, 1984.

Dawidowicz, Lucy S. *On Equal Terms: Jews in America, 1881–1981.* New York: Holt, Rinehart & Winston, 1982.

de Lange, Nicholas. *Atlas of the Jewish World.* New York: Facts on File Publications, 1984.

Greenberg, Martin H. *The Jewish Lists.* New York: Schocken Books, 1979.

Howe, Irving. *World of Our Fathers.* New York: Simon & Schuster, 1976.

Karp, Abraham J. *Golden Door to America: The Jewish Immigrant Experience.* New York: Viking Press, 1976.

———. *Haven and Home: A History of the Jews in America.* New York: Schocken Books, 1985.

Plesure, Milton. *Jewish Life in Twentieth-Century America: Challenge and Accommodation.* Chicago: Nelson-Hall, 1982.

Silberman, Charles E. *A Certain People: American Jews and Their Lives Today.* New York: Summit Books, 1985.

Villiers, Douglas, ed. *Next Year in Jerusalem: Portraits of the Jew in the Twentieth Century.* New York: Viking Press, 1976.

INDEX

PICTURE CREDITS

HOWARD MUGGAMIN is a lecturer on 20th-century studies with a special interest in Jewish-American culture. A frequent contributor to scholarly journals and other publications, he divides his time between New York City, Los Angeles, and Akron, Ohio.

DANIEL PATRICK MOYNIHAN is the senior United States senator from New York. He is also the only person in American history to serve in the cabinets or subcabinets of four successive presidents—Kennedy, Johnson, Nixon, and Ford. Formerly a professor of government at Harvard University, he has written and edited many books, including *Beyond the Melting Pot, Ethnicity: Theory and Experience* (both with Nathan Glazer), *Loyalties,* and *Family and Nation.*